GOALKEEPING

Also by Bob Wilson

BOB WILSON – AN AUTOBIOGRAPHY

GOALKEEPING

BOB WILSON
(Arsenal F.C.)

PELHAM BOOKS

First published in Great Britain by
PELHAM BOOKS LTD
52 *Bedford Square*
London WC1B 3EF
NOVEMBER 1970
SECOND IMPRESSION DECEMBER 1971
THIRD IMPRESSION JUNE 1973
FOURTH IMPRESSION DECEMBER 1976

© 1970 *by Bob Wilson*

All Rights Reserved. No part of this publication may be reproduced, stored in a retrieval system, or transmitted, in any form or by any means, electronic, mechanical, photocopying, recording or otherwise, without the prior permission of the Copyright owner

ISBN 0 7207 0337 9

Printed lithographically in Great Britain by Hollen Street Press Ltd, at Slough and bound by Redwood Burn at Esher, Surrey

CONTENTS

INTRODUCTION 9

1 IMPORTANCE OF A GOALKEEPER 11
General – as a defender – as an observer passing forward information – as a director and tactician.

2 PERSONAL QUALITIES 27
Height – weight – hands – strength – fitness – agility – mobility – reaction – safe handling – positional sense – anticipation – courage and fearlessness – concentration – confidence – nerves and mental attitude – speed of movement.

3 ACCEPTED TECHNIQUES 43
Basic position – the high ball – position of 'keeper in relation to crosses – deflecting a high ball – knee up – punching – catching a waist-high ball – the low shot – diving for shots to the side – ground shots – diving at a forward's feet – approaching out of goal – penalties – passing back – making a clearance and four-step rule – clearances: throwing and kicking – conclusion.

4 THE PSYCHOLOGY OF GOALKEEPING 69
Study of opponents (1) before the game (2) during the game – elimination of possibilities (1) reading the situation (2) forcing errors upon an opponent.

5 FUNCTIONAL TRAINING 75
Situation training – personal training programme – exercises and activities.

6 INTRODUCTION OF GOALKEEPING IN SCHOOL 95
Games from primary school age up to secondary school age.

7 IN RETROSPECT 105
Great goalkeepers.

ILLUSTRATIONS

between pages 64 and 65

The basic position for a goalkeeper

Here Bob Wilson uses his fist to clear from the heads of Nottingham Forest forwards

Bob Wilson shows how a goalkeeper should position himself to take a low shot

Liverpool's Tommy Lawrence, who Bob Wilson rates as one of the bravest goalkeepers in the country, grabs the ball from the foot of Chelsea's Birchenall

Bob Wilson demonstrates an exercise which strengthens stomach muscles and punching ability

This picture strip illustrates how Bob Wilson quickens his reactions by having to lay flat by the post before a server throws or kicks the ball to the other side of the goal

These series of pictures show the sitting, kneeling and squatting positions in Bob Wilson's special training programme

England's Gordon Banks, who Bob Wilson rates as one of the best goalkeepers the country has ever produced, seen in action against Scotland at Wembley

Derby County goalkeeper Les Green, high in Bob Wilson's list of the country's most promising young 'keepers, makes a spectacular dive, but could not stop this free-kick from Burnley winger Dave Thomas from going into the net

ACKNOWLEDGEMENT

Some of the diagrams and drawings in this book are reproduced from an F.A. coaching book by kind permission of the Football Association.

INTRODUCTION

GOALKEEPING MAY APPEAR ON THE SURFACE TO BE A RATHER uninteresting and vague topic upon which to base a book. But, in fact, the subject of the goalkeeper comprises not only interesting material and information but also it can become a subject to which in certain respects there is no ending and no answer.

As there are no detailed works on the art of goalkeeping I had a special reason for attempting to tread uncovered ground. Several noted authorities on the art of goalkeeping have been referred to such as the late Frank Swift, and of more recent fame, Ron Springett and present First Division goalkeepers.

I have gone into practically every aspect of keeping goal, ranging from essential qualities and accepted techniques to functional training and the psychology of goalkeeping.

The subject, psychology may already change the conception of a goalkeeper in the reader's mind, for I find the average person considers the man between the posts to be short of intelligence and slightly mad. A few goalkeepers have a crazy courageous streak, but in an era when a scientific approach is taken, the goalkeeper uses intelligence as well as instinct and acrobatic skill to keep the ball out of the one hundred and ninety-two square feet of his goal.

If you doubt the worth of a goalkeeper, I hope the ensuing chapters will change your mind, or at least rid you of the illusion of the crazy man, which isn't quite true!

More than one good 'keeper would agree with the traditional 'crazy' theory. John Osborne, who kept goal for

West Bromwich Albion against Everton in the 1968 F.A. Cup Final, says: 'You have to be slightly mental, I think. After all you have selected a job which is like being "tail end Charlie" in a bomber. You're there to be shot at.'

1. IMPORTANCE OF A GOALKEEPER

General – As a defender – As an observer passing forward information – As a director and tactician.

I BELIEVE IT'S ESSENTIAL TO PUT THE IMPORTANCE OF A goalkeeper in its correct perspective immediately. In this case my first chapter deals with his importance from four viewpoints.

(a) *General*

There is one position on the field where ball control will not do you any good and that is between the sticks, where you may be a hero one day and less than the dust the next.

The uprights and cross-bar of the soccer goal enclose an area of one hundred and ninety-two square feet and even if you are not very good at figures that's still an awful lot of feet. Of course, it may not seem very much if you happen to be a forward but if you're the chap in sweater and cap who has the unenviable job of keeping the ball out, that yawning space can seem as big as Wembley Stadium.

However, all 'keepers know they have chosen a 'glamour' position but because mistakes are crucial and isolated they certainly pay for the privilege.

Soccer is a game of split second decisions. Forwards must make them, backs must make them, but on nobody do they descend as suddenly and frequently as on the goalkeeper! Should he catch the ball or punch it away? Sould he stay on his line or come out to intercept? Questions like these are with him all the time. In certain situations there are obvious principles to follow, one thing and one thing only to be done. But at other times he has to make up his mind on the spur of the moment, and hope that he has made it correctly! I need hardly say that these occasions are probably in the majority.

That is one reason why it is difficult to write about goalkeeping. Much of it is simply instinct and common sense.

Fig. 1. 'Much of it is simply instinct and common sense'

Laying down hard and fast rules is dangerous, because as often as not, you never know quite what is going to happen until it is actually happening.

How often is it said that 'goalkeeping is the easiest job of any player'. These sceptics are thinking of the days when the goalkeeper is relatively inactive and therefore to them, all he is doing is making up the team. But this is only one of the psychological hazards of keeping goal. You are often left in the cold for periods on the line and are then suddenly expected to pull out a wonder save.

IMPORTANCE OF A GOALKEEPER

I have found the need to keep my concentration mentally exhausting and one of the most tiring aspects of 'keeping.

These are a few of the reasons why, when teams are picked for a game of football at school or in the park the inevitable question arises – 'Well who is going in goal?' Usually it ends up being the worst player or most timid. It is easy to understand, for sometimes you feel rather left out of things between the goalposts and everyone prefers to be a Bobby Charlton or Denis Law in schoolboy kick-abouts.

(b) *Importance as a defender*

I need say very little on this aspect because everyone realises that in defence no one man is as important as a goalkeeper. When everyone else has failed to counter an attack, the onus falls ultimately on the goalkeeper. Then he becomes a hero or scorn is poured on his failure.

If there is one thing I have learned from watching and from my own coaching, it is that the successful teams are strong right down the middle and by that I mean in goal, at centre-half, full-back, and in the frontal striking position.

The two former – i.e. goalkeeper and centre-half-back or full-backs work in close collaboration. If there is a weakness in one defender, then the other begins to show doubts in his own ability.

An example was Pat Jennings, the Spurs keeper who looked shaky on crosses, after Maurice Norman's injury, but became ultra-confident when Mike England arrived at Tottenham.

Basically it is the psychological knowledge that if you go and fail to gather a high cross the good centre-half is covering.

I am a strong believer in the feeling that a team's confidence stems from its defensive covering. If the 'keeper is seemingly impregnable in the early stages of the game, it has a considerable psychological effect on the team. He can, in fact, instil or ruin the confidence and prospects of any team.

In any other defensive position, or for that matter any attacking position, there are times when mistakes are made which do not have any impact on the game. But the goalkeeper who has a brilliant game for 89 minutes and in the 90th misjudges a shot, which results in a goal and a defeat, has no help and is looked on as having let the team down and causing defeat.

This is what I meant when I said in the introduction that 'keepers pay for the privilege of the glamour position.

The Brazilian coach, after his team won the World Cup Final in Sweden in 1958, was asked to comment on his team's success. He replied: 'A brilliant save by the goalkeeper is every bit as important as a scoring shot at the other end. Yet the 'keeper is seldom the subject of back-slapping'.

How true this is. But conversely I would say that the forward who misses an easy chance has committed as bad a crime as the unfortunate 'keeper.

Of course, the importance of a goalkeeper does not end here, for not only is he the last line of defence but he is also the first stage of the attack.

And also being behind every member of his team he can observe the formations of not only his team, but his opponents. These are now covered in points (c) and (d).

(c) *Importance as an observer*

Undoubtedly the goalkeeper can play an extremely important part purely as an observer. Firstly, he is the rearguard of the team and as such can observe his ten colleagues as they either thrust into attack or back pedal to thwart an attack. He can, in fact, watch all twenty-one other players.

From his isolated position he is able to consider whether his defence is covering correctly, especially in complicated systems. Even with a simple diagonal defence it is his job to instruct his colleagues as to whether they are too central or too far out. I have found that more than once a shout of warning to one of the Arsenal back four, as to unseen danger has helped consolidate that near impregnable wall.

In a lesser way he is able to pass information forward if he can see why an attack is breaking down. A quick word can help correct simple faults.

Similarly, if his defence is being constantly split or penetrated, the goalkeeper is in the best position to see why it is failing. He can note quicker than any other member of the defence where the most dangerous opposition forward is and who he is.

His job as an observer can be carried to giving instructions to his defence. For example, if his left full-back is gathering the ball near a touch line, having his back to play, it is the goalkeeper who can survey the situation and warn him of an approaching player. Small as the point may appear, it plays an integral part of the team system and team confidence. All top level players will heartily endorse the importance of the 'keeper's shouts.

(d) *Importance as a director and tactician*

Although stopping goals is the first objective of keeping goal, it cannot be too strongly emphasised that a team benefits if the goalkeeper is able to begin an attacking movement with every clearance. If he kicks or throws the ball aimlessly, he is wasting creative openings and probably increasing his own work.

More often than not a hasty aimless clearance comes straight back and the overworked defence is unable to regain the composure that is essential if the team is to work as a unit. It took me quite a while to appreciate the usefulness of taking my time over clearances in certain situations.

Another point is that it requires considerable confidence to hold on indefinitely and judge when your team is composed or at least has had a 'breather' after heavy pressure.

The problem is 'when do I hold, when do I throw and, when do I kick'. If the 'keeper throws a ball every time to one particular position, he is making it obvious to the opposition, and recreating danger and we are back to square one, i.e. under pressure. Therefore he must find a compromise, whereby a throw and a kick can be used to equal and varying advantage. The various techniques of kicking and throwing a ball are covered in Chapter Three; but it is from these points that the 'keeper's real importance as a director and tactician emerge.

On some days he will exploit weather conditions and use the kick practically the whole time.

For instance in the case of a strong sun, into which the opposing defence are constantly looking, the high ball is ideal, and it is the goalkeeper who must realise the potential danger from such a ball, and adapt himself accordingly.

Likewise a throw will very often be of greater value than a kick, especially in strong winds and it is up to the 'keeper to determine which is having the best effect, and creating the better openings.

Further than this purpose of beginning attacks, I believe that the defence should be marshalled and directed by either the captain in one of the defensive positions or the centre-half. I do not think the goalkeeper should be the specific director, although he can help.

Everyone helps each other in the modern game but there is one area where the 'keeper is the boss. This is the six yard area. He must have complete authority and control of this area, and it is his own property, which he must guard with his life against all potential oppressors.

From a corner-kick he must place his men as he wants them and not as they wish. And the best way is to have the right full-back on the right-hand post, and the left full-back on the left-hand post. And these two are the only two defenders who are in this area. His centre-half should be just on the edge and in a position to counter any ball landing near the penalty spot.

I am more firmly convinced of this since encountering the famous or infamous tactics of Jackie Charlton who has been copied by all and sundry. And why not? Here is a loophole in the laws in my opinion.

I have always thought that such tactics constitute a foul, under rule 12 which states: 'That a player who trips an opponent, i.e. by throwing or attempting to throw him by the use of legs or by stooping in front of or behind him shall be penalised by the award of a direct free-kick.'

There is no doubt whatsoever in my mind that it is blatant obstruction. This is not sour grapes. Good luck to all who practise it. It is up to the goalkeeper to counteract it as it is obviously considered legal by most referees. I am the first to cheer if Arsenal score as a result of the tactic.

So remember when the ball is coming in make sure that it is a straight battle between the attacker and the 'keeper. Further if a second attacker is in range – i.e., one in front and one behind – then pray that the much maligned referee is not a ball watcher and that he really does know his job.

A 'keeper should not try to catch the ball unless he has at least three yards to move towards it. Instead he should get as big an area of body, i.e., usually hands behind it and have defenders keyed up for loose balls. If that ball is in the right place you have done a hell of a job just to keep it out of the net.

Finally, if you get the chance to punch out, try and clear the box; i.e. 18 yards.

Make no mistake, the first priority of Jackie and the rest is not to head the ball but to use arms, legs and body to prevent the 'keeper getting a clear view to punch or catch.

How to counteract it? It is most important that the 'keeper should organise his defence and get any colleague who is standing with the offending player to clear out to the edge of the box or beyond.

This gives the 'keeper more manoeuvrability and more space to attack the inswinging corner. Keep your full-backs with you on or around the part of the line that you are vacating.

It should be stressed that if an inswinging corner is accurately placed, as it often is by the Leeds perfectionists, then the 'keeper apart from trying to put into effect all his techniques of punching or catching must pray that the Gods are with him. He must hope that he can get at least a hand or a finger to it and then alert his defenders to the possibility of a loose ball.

If any high cross is floated into the six-yard area, it must

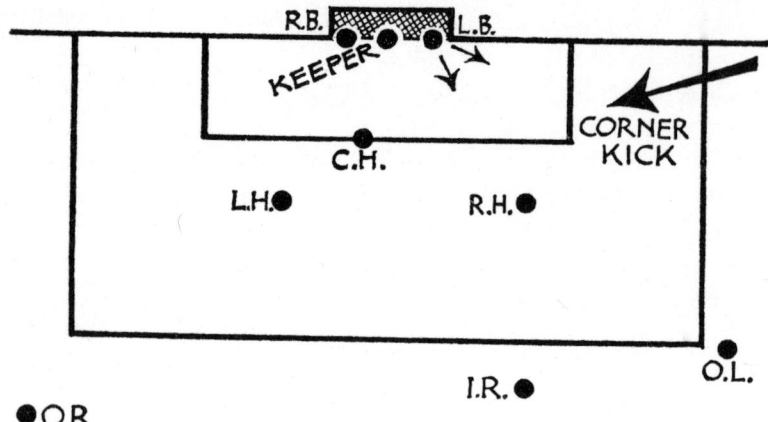

Fig. 2. The ideal positioning for the defence awaiting a corner

be his automatic function to call clearly for it and without hesitation move out to catch it. There are no half-measures. He must go.

Fig. 2 shows the ideal positioning for the defence awaiting a corner, i.e. the conventional corner with no complications such as crowding of the near post or a Charlton corner.

This does not just apply to a corner-kick but for any ball approaching the six-yard area. One of my commandments of goalkeeping is: 'Thou shalt have complete control in the six-yard area and 90 per cent control of the rest of the box, up to and just beyond the eighteen-yard area.'

Although I have stated that the overall area is in the authority of another more mobile defender, I am still a believer in the goalkeeper advising, but in this case he acts as an observer more than a director, and this is covered in point (c).

The only other specific directing any goalkeeper does or should do is that concerning line-ups for fouls.

Again in this age of initiative, the class player seeing a 'keeper lining up a wall, will take a quick shot and often succeed. At Arsenal we designate one player, usually a forward, to do the lining up, and I check that the cover is in my two

IMPORTANCE OF A GOALKEEPER

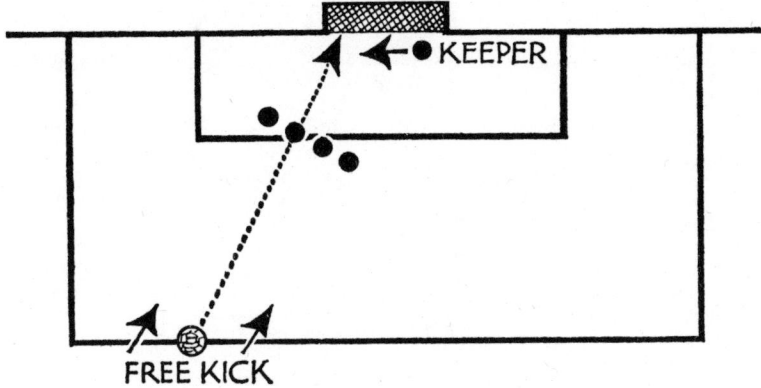

Fig. 3. Lining up the defence for a free kick

interests, i.e., (a) the side of the goal that I'm not covering; (b) that I have a clear view of it.

This organisation of free-kicks should be practised in training sessions and kept fresh in the mind by running through the tactics every week or so.

In the free-kick situation the 'keeper should be able to rely on a well-trained and marshalled team, and he must be able to read the situation immediately.

It is possible to instance the free-kicks.

(a) *Free kick at an angle, from the edge of the area*

This free-kick from any angle to the side of the goal calls for a strong line-up, with at least four players in the 'human wall'. They should comprise the full-back, responsible for this particular section of the field, a half-back and two forwards. They should be linked together firmly so there is no possibility of the wall breaking. The player who has lined up the wall, joins it in the angled free-kick, but there is a slight gap between him and his fellow defenders. Instead he positions himself on the far post and the 'keeper fills in the gap and tries to get into as central a position of his goal as is possible.

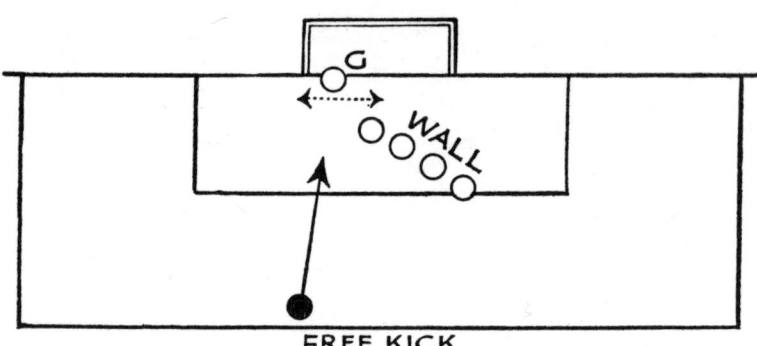

FREE KICK

Fig. 4. An alternative line-up – almost in reverse of Fig. 3

By far the best method of lining them up for this free-kick is to place the full-back in line with the post and ball (i.e. along the dotted line in Fig. 3). The other players form up to join him and the goalkeeper positions himself in the remaining gap.

But he must not be content in believing the wall is impregnable. He must be on the alert to cover any ball that gets through the wall, and more especially any clever chip or lob over the heads of the wall.

An alternative line-up in this situation is one almost in reverse of the above. This time, the wall covers the far side of the goal, which the 'keeper covers in the above, and the 'keeper guards the now more obvious gap in line with the ball. (Fig. 4)

This situation is more dangerous as it encourages a direct shot far more and renders the goal more easy for a chip, in that the angle is increased for a chip shot. Although I am uneasy about this line-up, Jack Kelsey ex-Wales and Arsenal goalkeeper is a great advocate of it and claims that only one goal was scored against him in all the time he used it when he was Arsenal's 'keeper.

I feel that clubs with any insight would soon spot what was happening and invent a means of exploiting the defensive

IMPORTANCE OF A GOALKEEPER

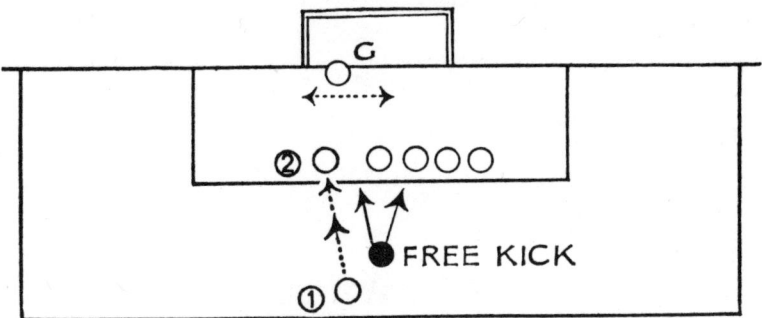

Fig. 5. Guarding the 'keeper during a free kick

line-up. And with powerful marksmen around like Francis Lee, this tactic becomes a similar situation to a full-back showing the line to Peter Thompson.

(b) *Free kick in front of goal*

For this most difficult free-kick, two methods especially are recommended :

(1) One is to place the wall, as Fig. 5 to guard one side of goal and leave the other side in the care of the 'keeper. The wall should include one more player making a total of five.

Again the player who lines up the wall '1', positions himself with the far post '2' and the 'keeper is central and between the gap. The same problems exist as in the previous type foul.

(2) The other method is to split the wall so that two players cover one side and three cover the other (Fig. 6). The middle portion is then left to the 'keeper. An additional problem occurs here in that the clever player will hit the ball to the inside of the player in the wall, on either side of the goal, and deflections are possible. An alert player will pounce to take advantage of the loose ball.

With this reservation or warning this method is quite sound.

GOALKEEPING

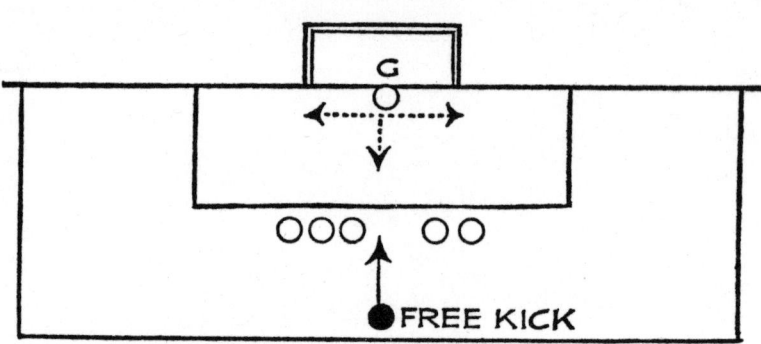

Fig. 6. Another method of protecting the goalkeeper

(c) *Free-kick close to goal* (Indirect)

For this type of free-kick, close to goal, only one method is used and that is for all members of the team to come back on to the goal line. And that means all eleven.

I was able to take part in an F.A. coaching experiment with this type of free kick, in which as soon as the ball was touched all players defending converged towards it. And out of about forty attempts no goal was forthcoming. This method is very good.

The goalkeeper's position should be in the middle and slightly in front of his fellows as in Fig. 7.

Positioning himself slightly in front of the rest of the team and certainly nearest to the ball, a 'keeper must be extra alert and courageous.

In all these cases and for any free-kick in the goal region the 'keeper is the tactician and director. He must, as I stated before, have practised all such moves intricately in training. Like most things in goalkeeping it should be automatic action.

One further important aspect in directing, linked closely with tactics, is the 'keeper's observance of his particular team's defensive pattern. Nowadays we no longer have just a traditional W.M. formation but diagonal; Swiss bolt, 4–2–4, and 4–3–3, to name but a few.

IMPORTANCE OF A GOALKEEPER

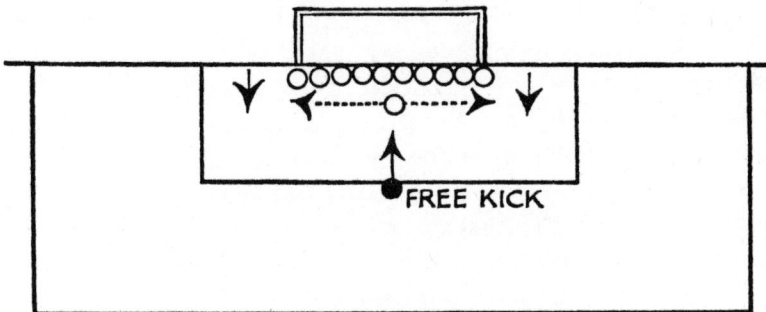

Fig. 7. Positioning for a free kick close to goal

Practised as they may be, there are games when things go wrong and the first to spot it should be the 'keeper. He therefore directs his colleagues with advice to retreat more, or move into the tackle quicker and so on.

In this way, a goalkeeper, if intelligent enough to assess the faults, can rapidly avert threatening danger.

We have seen how the 'keeper can act as director and tactician in defence. What about the forward line? Has he any contribution to make in this section? I can only point out the ways in which the 'keeper can direct attack by his throws or kicks. These are listed in the chapter on Techniques, but their use is underlined now:

(a) Short 'Water polo throw' – to a full-back, half-back or deep lying forward. Very accurate and powerful wrist movement.

(b) Over-arm throw – for distance; less accurate and liable to spin but can effectively change direction at speed.

(c) Punt – for distance, into the sun or with the wind. Can be dangerous if used properly, and not just to clear one's lines. It is particularly effective when the opposition are facing the sun.

(d) Half-volley – more accurate, less height; powerful: Can only be used in complete openings. High degree of skill needed.

In these throws and kicks the 'keeper can provide some tactical assault and direct the play of his forwards.

GOALKEEPING

In concluding this chapter let me say that although the above mentioned tips all go to make up the great 'keeper, everyone has faults and weaknesses. The schoolboy, in particular, should be aiming for ultimate perfection in his art and he must first and foremost get his priorities right.

The greatest priority is to keep that bladder of air out of his rigging. If he does that consistently well, he is a good 'keeper. He is a great 'keeper if he can combine all the other attributes that give him his position of importance.

2. PERSONAL QUALITIES

Height – Weight – Hands – Strength – Fitness – Agility – Mobility – Reaction – Safe Handling – Positional Sense – Anticipation – Courage and Fearlessness – Concentration – Confidence – Nerves and Mental Attitude – Speed of Movement

IN THIS CHAPTER I WILL LIST THE ESSENTIAL QUALITIES and aspects that go to make a good goalkeeper. This is not to say that without the following qualities a certain goalkeeper is not efficient. Indeed, when one stresses height as a contributory factor one only has to think of the height of some of England's goalkeepers. Hopkinson (Bolton) at 5 ft. 8 in.; Hodgkinson (Sheffield United), 5 ft. 8½; Ron Springett (Sheffield Wednesday), only 5 ft. 9½ in.

In my opinion, the fact that Hopkinson and Hodgkinson were unable to hold their places in the England team was due to their lack of inches. It makes me wonder if the days of the 6 ft. 2 in. goalkeeper such as Frank Swift are gone!

What I am aiming for in this chapter is to present a picture of the ideal goalkeeper both physically and mentally.

Height

If one begins on the essential physical qualities, one immediately imagines a keeper to be tall. Undoubtedly a six-foot tall goalkeeper, if he has the necessary agility, has an immense advantage over the smaller man.

For high cross balls especially, those extra inches make the task more simple, and similarly one often sees a small 'keeper dive full-length and acrobatically turn a ball away, where in fact a tall agile 'keeper would be able to grasp the shot firmly and far more easily.

This, in my opinion, is the reason for the small goalkeepers England fielded in the early 1960's. In an age of soccer dominated by the continental approach, the spectacular 'keeper often is appreciated more than the safe. If nothing else, it attracts the smaller boy to take up goalkeeping. And we can no longer quote Frank Swift, who said: 'The tallest goalkeepers are not always the best, but the great majority of first-class goalkeepers in Britain are at least 5 ft. 10 in.'

I get quite a few letters from young lads telling me that they are only such and such in height and do I think they have any chance, being so small?

I always tell them they have a chance, but only if they develop the assets accruing from their lack of inches. These are usually more suppleness, greater natural agility and more gymnastic physique. But I do stress that most important of all – you have to develop to the highest degree, footwork, speed of movement and positional play. In my opinion this is the only possible way to counteract those lack of inches.

For my ideal 'keeper I would like a six-foot man in possession, assuming he has the required agility and speed of movement. to go with it.

Some time ago an experiment was carried out, using three goalkeepers, a schoolboy aged 14 (5 ft.), a tall boy of 17 (5 ft. 10 in.) and an international goalkeeper 5 ft. $9\frac{1}{2}$ in.). Each was filmed in slow motion, leaping to stop three kinds of shot:

(i) – immediately overhead,

(ii) – making for the top corner of the net,

(iii) – making for the base of the upright.

In figures 8, 9 and 10 limits of reach are plotted for each player. You can see that the top corner of the goal is out of reach of a goalkeeper in his jump from a standing position in the middle of the goal.

The speeds of movement were also calculated and the times of the international goalkeeper were 1.2/64 sec. to reach overhead, 1.9/64 sec. to reach corner and 1.13/64 sec. to reach corner and 1.13/64 sec. horizontal. Reach in jumping and speed of reaction are therefore very valuable assets in a goalkeeper.

Weight

While considering height, it is worthwhile mentioning weight, but this cannot be specific, for many large men are quite nimble

PERSONAL QUALITIES

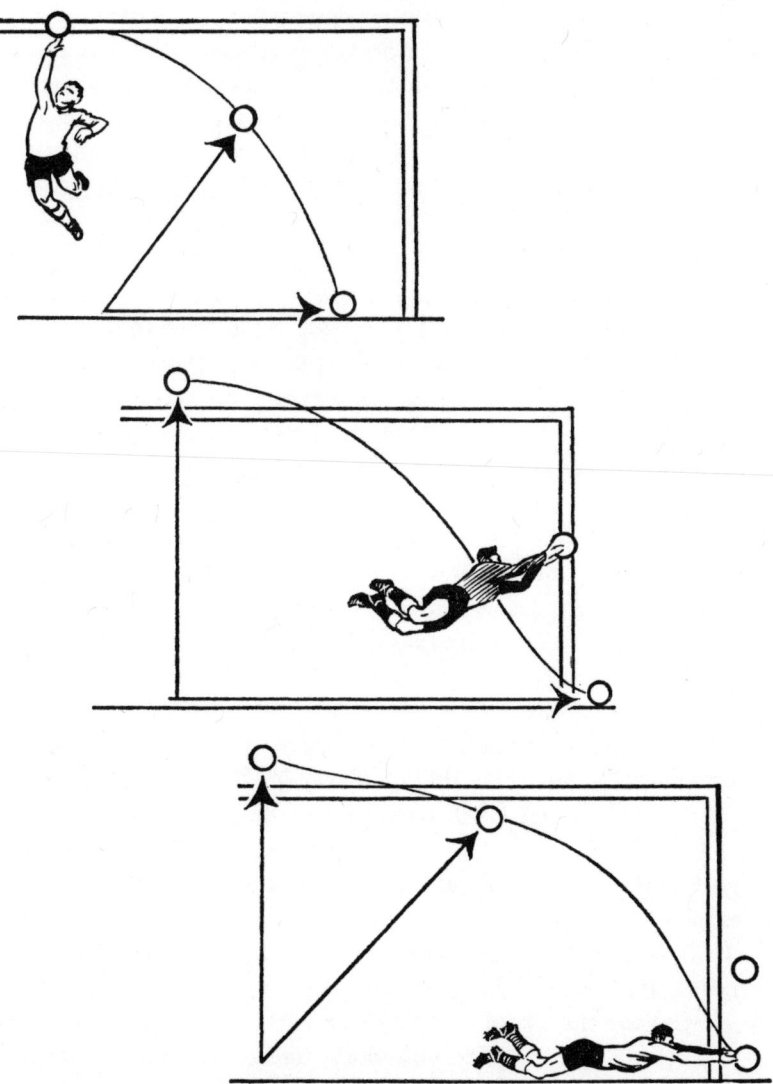

Fig. 8, 9, 10. (*Top*) Limits of reach of a 14-year-old schoolboy. (*Middle*) Limits of reach of a young goalkeeper (5ft 10in.). (*Bottom*) Limits of reach of an international goalkeeper (5ft 9½in.)

on their feet. However, I have no doubt that a 15-stone 'keeper must find greater difficulty, especially with low shots. It seems incredible that Sheffield United once possessed a goalkeeper, William Foulkes, who stood six-feet tall and weighed 22 stones. And he played for England! The ideal for a six-foot goalkeeper is between 12 stone 6 lb. and 13 stone 6 lb. and scaled down accordingly.

Hands

A brief word should be said about hands for they are the most important part of the goalkeeper's equipment. They, of course, indicate his specialist position on the field. Is it important to have large hands? This question is often asked in connection with goalkeepers, and again one can only theorise and state that it must be advantageous. The great Frank Swift, for instance, had a huge hand, measuring $11\frac{3}{4}$ inches, from his little finger to the tip of his thumb. And nowadays Pat Jennings of Spurs has a huge pair of hands. Ultimately it is not how *large* they are but how *safe* they are.

Strength

Little emphasis need be placed on a goalkeeper's strength. It is generally accepted that goalkeepers have a general level of fitness and indeed I will mention this shortly. More especially they have a specific type of fitness, for their work is of a different type to that of the ball player and different muscle groups are involved.

In training the 'keeper, whether he is a professional, amateur or schoolboy, should have at least two sessions a week devoted to developing the various qualities that he as a specialist requires – i.e., suppleness, agility, mobility, etc., etc. These are all covered in the training chapter in this book.

However, if a goalkeeper has got strength it will not have a derogatory effect. Indeed it will be useful, for strength and stamina go hand in glove. It is useful in throwing for distance; in kicking both a dead ball and a ball from the hands. And stamina is required to overcome constant attacking by the opposition and more especially to counteract the mud-patches and heavy grounds that are part and parcel of English soccer.

Strength also gives the 'keeper that powerful spring to get clear of the mud, to get airborne and achieve those vital inches which enable him to catch the ball.

Additionally, with so much physical contact, especially from corner-kicks and cross-balls, this strength is vital and can make the difference between clinging on to the ball or having it knocked away.

Fitness

The goalkeeper is often the centre of discussion as regards fitness. 'He doesn't need to be as fit as the normal player' is often exclaimed. I disagree with this statement, but then I disagree with the people who train goalkeepers alongside the players solely and without specialist treatment and sessions, such as are described in the training chapter.

As I have stated in the section on strength, a goalkeeper needs specific fitness, based on the type of work and movements he has to perform. I will not go into the training needed to develop fitness for goalkeepers for this is covered in Chapter 5. Suffice to say that suppleness, mobility and agility fitness is required especially; far more than the outfield player. Training in these aspects is stressed together with spring and strength in legs. These are invaluable, and if combined with a degree of the general players' training, give the keeper a fitness that is by no means inferior to anyone else's, but more especially is ideal for his job.

Agility

Undoubtedly one of the more important arts of goalkeeping is the ability to throw the body into varying positions at speed. This is basically instinctive, but the natural agility has to be sharpened by constant training and practice.

You cannot be a good 'keeper without this ability, and the class 'keeper is able to hurl his weight on towards or after the ball at speed.

Mobility

Some people would consider that mobility is the same as agility. Of course, agility and mobility are very closely allied, but are nevertheless different.

One may often observe a young 'keeper, or League goalkeeper for that matter, showing remarkable agility and not consider whether he could have avoided the spectacular by using his feet. A fault of all too many 'keepers is that they lack mobility, yet have agility. Some do it purposefully, to be continental and to look good! And vice-versa. To be a good goalkeeper the two attributes must be present.

Footwork and quickness off the mark is mobility as far as the keeper is concerned.

Speed and quickness off the mark is vital. Once the decision is made to go for the ball, getting there and the time it takes are all important. In training the 'keeper should try and develop his speed off the mark to the highest degree.

In general, it is necessary to be fast over a distance from five to ten yards, although the keeper can often act as an extra outfield defender. A fast sprint from his goal area can cut out any danger from a through ball, which the 'keeper fly-kicks away.

Finally, no one doubts the fact that the safe is far better than the spectacular and by good mobility, combined with agility, the budding goalkeeper is halfway to success.

Reaction

This is an aspect and quality that has to be built up and improved by training and practice, and to some extent experience.

A player should be trained to the extent that a shot from close range or a shot diverted is not lost, but can be recovered and saved by an automatic reaction. Many people say this is instinct. Indeed, I agree, but virtually all goalkeeping is instinct, and this particular instinct can be sharpened by training such as squash, five-a-side games and pressure training. More about these exercises in Chapter 5.

Safe Handling

The handling of a ball by the goalkeeper either creates or destroys the confidence of the defence. If he is constantly fumbling high balls or low balls, then the defence begins to mistrust him and will kick aimlessly away or miskick themselves. But if he shouts confidently and fields a ball in the same manner, the defence moves with an air of supreme understanding. And this, I believe, transfers to the forwards as well. In fact, to the whole team.

Most experienced goalkeepers will stress the desire to 'catch always rather than punch' and this is true. Experience and judgement alone will tell you whether that high ball close to the bar should be caught or turned over. In this case, with the danger of being bustled into the net, it should be turned over. 'Safety first' is always the goalkeeper's motto.

At this point in the chapter I would like to stress that all these qualities are gifts to a great extent. Unless you are gifted in this way, it would be pointless taking up goalkeeping in the first place. But all these abilities can be learned and developed by the person who really gives his mind to it.

Positional sense and anticipation

You may feel that it is impossible to *learn* the art of anticipation; the art of guessing what your opponents are going to do in the next ten movements. Not at all! For a start you should make a practice of mentally 'putting yourself in the other man's shoes' when danger threatens.

Imagine for a moment that you are an inside-forward with the ball bearing down on the goal. The centre-forward is coming up behind you, having outdistanced the centre-half. As a sensible player, would you try to dribble round the back, or would you pass back to the unmarked centre-forward some ten yards away? The answer is obvious, isn't it? Now come back to goalkeeping, facing a situation as described above. You should clearly be able to anticipate that the real threat will come from the centre-forward and so move accordingly.

The example is a very simple and elementary one, but the principle is sound. If you want to know what a player is going to do then credit him with as much intelligence as you have yourself, and what you would do, if in his boots.

Of course you won't be right every time, but at least you can come off a lot better than if no thought was given to the matter. Naturally, everything depends on the speed with which you can put yourself in the other fellow's place and guess what he is going to do. With practice you should hardly have to think about it, for it will become an automatic reaction.

Positional sense and anticipation are closely allied. Positional sense is essential in that the goalkeeper must at all times know where he stands in relation to his goal.

You used to be able to mark your six-yard box, but now it is judged illegal (although many 'keepers still continue to do it). So nowadays it is more and more essential that by experience you are aware at all times of your own position in relation to the goal.

The only set mark a 'keeper can cast a glance at is the penalty-spot. Until you become supremely confident in your positional sense, it is advisable during practice or actual games to keep glancing at your position in relation to the near or far post and imagine whether you could be beaten easily if a forward was facing you.

Angles

This is best exemplified by placing yourself in an outfield position. Imagine that a forward has the ball on the corner of the six-yard line and is about to shoot. If you stand right in the centre of your goal, then he will see a big space on one side of you and a small space on the other. This is bad goalkeeping. But if you move across your goal towards him and come out of your goal slightly then he will see only a small space on either side of you. To score, the forward will attempt to push the ball in the corners of the goal and it is your duty to make his task as difficult as possible. A goalkeeper must concentrate on the business of angles for its knowledge is invaluable.

If you are in any doubt, the ball should be placed on the penalty spot and you should imagine you are a forward about to shoot for goal. Then get a player to stand on the goal-line and you will see that you could place the ball in either corner quite easily.

Now this movement is repeated but the player stands on the six-yard line. You will find it much more difficult to score as he has narrowed the angle. It isn't so easy to put it into the corner because if it isn't exactly right you are going to put it within easy reach of the goalkeeper and he can stick his foot out and reach the ball.

Young goalkeepers are well advised to spend much time concentrating on the angles question. During practice and in matches, watch carefully the position of the forward as he shoots; make a study of it by coming out a few steps and moving across the goal a little. This makes it more difficult for him to score.

Other points to note on angles include the following:
(a) make yourself as big as possible when faced by an attacker;
(b) spread yourself – arms, shoulders, etc;
(c) you should be well-balanced – i.e., not moving forward, otherwise you will have no spring available;
(d) be on your toes ready to spring, dive or change direction.

Courage and Fearlessness

I have no hesitation in saying that these qualities are invaluable. Only if you have experienced the sensation of a huge forward bearing down on goal with just you to beat, can you realise the difficulty some people have in diving at players' feet.

But, like everything else, it must become instinctive and without any second thought. The person who thinks twice before going down is generally injured. This is not to say a 'keeper doesn't get injured by an instinctive dive. You do. But the number of times a 'keeper dives at the feet of a forward and escapes unscathed and saves a certain goal is in the majority. The action therefore, whatever anyone says, is justified.

Courage would be the first quality I would look for in any player, whether he is a goalkeeper or outfield player.

There is no place for the faint-hearted in the modern game and, just as forwards must be brave in tight tackling positions, so must the 'keeper have no second thought about throwing himself into flashing boots.

In my opinion, courage and fearlessness are essential qualities and I can only stress this by the saying that with this quality the difference is made between an average and a top-class goalkeeper.

Concentration

Have you ever watched those goalkeepers who, when the goal is not in immediate danger, spend time gazing idly around or even chat to spectators?

If you aim to be a goalkeeper, then you must start even before the whistle blows. Limbering up in the dressing-room is vital to get rid of any stiffness and to be adequately supple and mobile before going on to the pitch. Also, throwing a ball against a wall or having one thrown at you goes a long way to eliminating pre-match nerves.

More especially, when the 'kicking in' takes place, the goalkeeper must get used to the state of the pitch and judge the speed of balls off the surface whether it be wet or dry. He does this by asking his forwards to place balls where he wants them. Also he must work out his angles in relation to the lie of the pitch. This last point is important, for it often happens that in a goalmouth scramble a 'keeper loses all sense of direction and is not quite sure exactly of the position of his goal.

PERSONAL QUALITIES

Before he can work things out, the ball may well be in the net!

These aspects of concentration are essential and during the game I believe that the goalkeeper should follow play constantly. As I stated in the first chapter, it is his concentration and observation that enables him, better than other players, to 'read' the game, to detect deficiencies and assets and to be able to direct his colleagues.

I find home games at Arsenal in many ways far more difficult than away games. In away games you know that more often than not you are going to be under pressure, so you have no concentration problems.

But in home games you can be left 'out' of the game for long spells and if you are not careful the mind can wander. You have got to alert yourself to the fact that sooner or later your defence is going to fail you and then it will be up to you.

If you lose your concentration you inevitably fail to save, but if you retain that 'keyed' up feeling you are going to do your job more efficiently.

A goalkeeper must concentrate for the full 90 minutes, for one brief relaxation can spell defeat for your side.

Confidence

Little need be said on this aspect. A goalkeeper who lacks confidence in his own abilities should not be in the game. Confidence in goal, which is shown in several ways, undoubtedly communicates confidence to the whole team. One way is to display safe handling and another is by shouting instructions and encouragement.

This point of *shouting* is vital. Whenever the ball comes into the penalty area the goalkeeper should shout, especially if he wants it. Some people decry shouting within a team, yet a successful team is a team which co-operates one with another and this is done mostly by a shout. So a high ball into the six-yard area should be greeted by 'My ball, Jack,' and this shouting becomes so closely allied to confidence within, not only the defence, but the team.

Additionally, when an attack has failed against you or the defence has been under pressure, then it is the goalkeeper who wills the tired defenders to 'Get out' to 'Take them away.' The 'keeper is exhorting his team-mates to work hard to clear the immediate defensive area. He is anxious that they should take their rest on the halfway line and not on the edge of the 18-yard line.

I remember talking to Nobby Stiles about six months after Alex Stepney had been transferred to Manchester United. He told me how Alex shouted and encouraged his defenders and what a tremendous difference it had made to the team.

Nerves and Mental Attitude

A goalkeeper must have good nerves. The long periods of inactivity are especially trying and there is always the feeling that you may let through a simple goal. Other footballers may make many mistakes, but woe betide the 'keeper if he does.

Frank Swift, after a brilliant display at the age of 19 in a Cup Final, fainted as the final whistle blew and had to be revived. The nervous tension and strain had been too much.

If a goalkeeper lets two goals in fairly quickly he should not stop to worry or to deliberate where he went wrong, difficult though it may be. Instead he should concentrate on the next few shots and the rest of the game. He must realise that quite often it is another defender's fault.

Although it is important to have good nerves, it is not a bad thing to feel that funny sensation before games and to have misgivings about the coming game.

Gordon West of Everton, one of the best 'keepers in England, is sometimes physically sick with tension and nerves. But I guarantee that when he or any First Division 'keeper gets out on the park, they quickly lose the butterflies!

I have now completed what I believe to be the essential personal qualities of a goalkeeper. But there are other aspects and experience helps the 'keeper to make the correct decision.

Experience will tell him that he is only human and inevitably he will make mistakes on some days. *Every 'keeper makes mistakes. The good 'keepers are those who make the least errors.* This brings me back to the general outlook on goalkeeping, for on no other player does a mistake fall more heavily than the 'keeper.

Experience goes a long way in eradicating frequent mistakes and I feel that great 'keepers are at their best from the age of twenty-six onwards. Experience has taught them the difference between right and wrong.

Luck

A final vital factor in the success of a 'keeper is Lady Luck. Without it you let an impossible shot in, off the post. With it – you make an impossible save – off the post. It's as simple as that.

3. ACCEPTED TECHNIQUES

Basic position – the high ball – position of 'keeper in relation to crosses – deflecting a high ball – knee up – punching – catching a chest-high ball – catching a waist-high ball – the low shot – diving for shots to the side – ground shots – diving at a forward's feet – approaching out of goal – penalties – passing back or making a clearance and four-step rule – clearances: throwing and kicking – conclusion.

IN THIS CHAPTER ARE DESCRIBED THE MOST USED AND THE most difficult of the accepted techniques of goalkeeping. I have included modern ideas in line with the revolution in training methods.

Basic Position

The goalkeeper is required to dive, reach, jump or roll in the shortest possible time. In all the techniques explained in this chapter he must take up a position from which he will be able to save instantly.

The 'keeper's basic position should be with the feet slightly apart and knees slightly bent. The main part of his weight should be on the soles of his feet, with the immediate spring coming from the toes.

The body is bent forward with the arms forward and ready to pounce. Of course, the eyes must at all times be on the ball.

During a game a 'keeper should move around his area, following play. The basic position should be adopted when the play approaches his area.

The High Ball

Perhaps one of the most difficult saves a goalkeeper is called upon to make is the crossed high ball, which is usually a centre from either wing. Perfect balance, positioning and timing are required to cut out this danger and the save often has to be made when the area is crowded.

When and when not to go? These questions are answered by experience and constant practice, but one golden rule is paramount. That is 'the six yard area' is the goalkeeper's domain. All centres and corners within this area should be his

GOALKEEPING

Fig. 11. The high ball

responsibility. Additionally, the goalkeeper should always face the direction from which the ball is coming and when he thinks he has it covered or is within range, only then does the 'keeper leap out towards it.

'Keep your eye on the ball' is a rule that applies to every ball game, but in no phase of a game does it apply with more urgent force than that of the goalkeeper going out to catch a high ball. He has many temptations to take his eye off the ball for there are obstacles in his way, in the shape of well-meaning defenders and hostile attackers. He must resist the temptation

ACCEPTED TECHNIQUES

Fig. 12. The jump is obtained with a single foot take-off

to look at any of them and be prepared for the physical contact which must occur.

The goalkeeper should call when he is going out for a ball and his defenders should get out of his way, either marking a man or dropping back on to the goal line. They should be made aware of the possibility of a dropped ball and be ready to kick clear.

The flight of the ball must be judged precisely, and the goalkeeper must leap with power which requires good leg strength. The jump is obtained with a single foot take-off and the goalkeeper reaches up with both hands behind the ball, the fingers outspread.

If the shot is fierce, the goalkeeper allows his hands to recede, in order to take the pace from the ball. This is the same in a

GOALKEEPING

Fig. 13. The ball is watched right into the hands

shot gathered to the stomach. The tendency of young goalkeepers is to let the ball drop until they can clasp it to the chest, but this will enable forwards to get up and head the ball. The arm-length catch, however, if timed correctly should outreach any forward.

The ball is watched right into the hands and particular attention is necessary as the 'keeper jumps. As soon as the hands take the ball, the elbows bend to bring the ball quickly down in front of the body, and if possible clutched to the chest tight and secure and impossible to escape.

ACCEPTED TECHNIQUES

In today's overcrowded penalty areas the asset of courage is needed to decide to 'go' strongly and confidently and meet the challenge of physical contact.

One of the sure marks of a good goalkeeper is his safe fielding of high balls. With experience and confidence, the goalkeeper can venture beyond the six-yard area and take the weight from his defenders, by catching balls as far out as the penalty spot, dependent on where the ball is hit from.

If possible the high balls should always be taken as the 'keeper moves forward and upwards, although it is possible to save a high ball in a backward angled position.

Balls hit from touch lines or backward positions enable a 'keeper to get out beyond the penalty spot. The ball usually takes a fair time to reach its destination and the 'keeper has that extra time to get out.

The 'keeper has less chance to cut out a ball hit from close range crosses.

The 'keeper is dragged towards the near post and if a ball is crossed from these positions he literally has only a fraction of a second to intercept.

Positions of 'Keeper in Relation to Crosses

(1) For a ball hit from the touchline area a 'keeper should be central or backward of central so that he can move either towards the cross or back across to gather the centre.

(2) Centres closer to the goal tend to drag the 'keeper further towards the near post. The 'keeper has to move towards the near post to cover any attempted shot. A common pass in modern football is placed to the near post.

Deflecting a High Ball

'Keepers catching a high ball should beware of being charged by a forward as soon as they touch the ground. If a 'keeper is near the goal-line he will probably not catch the ball but deflect it.

There are many occasions when 'keepers are aware, when

GOALKEEPING

Fig. 14. Deflecting a high ball

going up for a high ball near their goal-line, that a forward is dangerously close. There is an element of risk involved in catching the ball and as a goalkeeper's motto is 'safety first' the obvious thing to do is to turn that kind of ball over the bar.

It is extremely unwise simply to flick the ball over the bar with the back of the hand. Instead young goalkeepers should always make sure by using the palms of both hands if possible.

ACCEPTED TECHNIQUES

Fig. 15. Punching clear a high ball

With experience and knowledge one hand can later be used. The advantage of the one-handed deflection is that the goalkeeper can obtain slightly more height than with both hands.

In both methods the palm of the hand is used, and not the back of the hand or a fist, to eliminate the danger of the ball slipping off the knuckles. The goalkeeper leaps high as for a caught ball and, as the ball touches the palm and fingers, the hand turns and literally guides the ball over the bar. If possible the ball should actually be contacted when it is higher than the crossbar.

For a fast shot going just under the bar both hands should

Fig. 16. A single-fisted punch

be used to gain an upward thrust through the jump. Again the hands are inclined backwards to guide the ball to safety.

Knee up

A final point in connection with high balls is that after springing from a one-footed take-off the 'keeper should try and get the opposite knee in a right-angle position. This affords him greater protection from a knock.

Punching

When several players jump for a ball together or the ball falls too far away from goal to catch it, experience alone will

ACCEPTED TECHNIQUES

Fig. 17. Double-handed punch

indicate whether it is advisable to punch it rather than try to catch it.

Again safety should be the motto and youngsters generally use a two-handed punch and try to punch in the direction they face. Ideally a 'keeper should always try to position himself so that he can punch a ball to the wings. This will give him time to get back to his goal even if it goes to an opponent. With experience a single-fisted punch is adequate and gives the 'keeper more height and a slightly stronger punch. The jump is the same as for high balls and a strong bent arm is used. With practice one will learn that a ball can be punched 20 yards or more with this bent arm punch. But it also has to be delivered *fast*, just as a javelin is thrown with a *fast* arm.

Catching a Chest-high Ball

Another golden rule of goalkeeping is always to get the body behind the ball. In catching a chest-high ball this is done and a clutching action is used. Allow the ball to meet the chest with two arms curled underneath it and tighten the fingers around it.

Some 'keepers find this type of catching unsafe in that the ball may bounce away. Therefore a second action is often used.

In this, one hand is placed above and one below, the elbows are kept close to the body and the fingers are outspread. This same action can be used for a ball caught under the chin. Experience allows both actions to be used.

Catching a Waist-high Ball

This is the easiest shot to catch, but it is often a powerful one. The goalkeeper must break the force of the ball by taking it with his hands and guiding it to his stomach. The hands are again held palm upwards so that the ball can be hugged to the chest. The ball may be taken either by the hands with the elbows slightly in front of the body, or into the lower chest with the elbows at the side and the hands wrapping over the ball. The ball should be caught against the body and the force taken out with a movement backwards.

The Low Shot

For this type of shot the goalkeeper positions himself directly in line with the oncoming ball. His legs should be kept almost together as he bends down to place the hands, palm upwards, under the ball. Some goalkeepers prefer to bend the legs a little, while others like to keep the legs almost straight.

In my opinion, the first position seems the best, especially if the goalkeeper has to move away quickly after he has held the ball. The elbows are turned inwards and immediately the hands take the ball they are brought towards the chest, the ball being clutched firmly.

Some goalkeepers crouch down in a sideways position to the approaching ball. They turn and half-kneel on the leg and the ball is scooped into the chest.

I would stress that low shots are always unwelcome, and more so if the ground is greasy. It will be recalled that Lewis, the Arsenal goalkeeper in 1926, confident of his low shot, allowed it to slip through his hands and over the line. That goal has been attributed to a new sweater but basic techniques and concentration would have prevented the goal. It is fatal for a goalkeeper to think there is any easy save, because every shot, if concentration is lax, could score.

Diving for Shots to the Side

These can be divided into shots –
(a) able to be covered by the body,
(b) at full arms length.

(a) The same principles as catching a ball to the chest apply when a goalkeeper has to dive to a ball that is easily within his reach. Always the goalkeeper should try to get his body behind the ball. However, it needs a great deal of practice. The same grip should be used as before, with one hand on top and one below. This ensures that the ball remains under control even after the impact of the ground. Catching the ball while at the same time falling sideways is an art which needs a lot of practice during training sessions. (See Plate 11)

(b) When a ball is out of reach of the body but just within reach of the hands the goalkeeper should always try to catch it. A ball that is only parried usually ends up as a goal.

It is often claimed that a tall goalkeeper is easily beaten by a low shot. Personally I think reach is still an advantage when dealing with these shots, the worst of which is the one that has to be taken at full stretch. Ability to deal with it comes from practice, which in turn brings confidence and skill in catching the ball. (See Plate 20)

Fig. 18. Dealing with a ground shot

However, the safety-first drill is the most important thought, so if a 'keeper is going to push this type of shot round the post he should push outwards as well as sideways, for otherwise the force of the shot may knock his hands back sufficiently for the ball to enter the net. (Fig 18)

To catch a ball, a strong and fast spring is required to place the body parallel to the ground. Usually the knees are slightly flexed. The arms are straight and the hands should be placed behind the ball and the top hand slightly on top of the ball. This both prevents the ball going through or bouncing back out.

To young goalkeepers the fact of diving and impact with the ground is in some respect frightening. But he should be assured that if he throws himself wholeheartedly after a ball he will never hurt himself, although on a hard ground a few grazes may occur. A ball held safely with no resulting goal eradicates any pain.

Ground Shots

Whenever a goalkeeper falls to the ground to hold a ball with his hands his first action should be to pull the ball quickly into his body. The ball then remains hugged to the chest while he rises and clears. All the same principles of safety catching apply (i.e., one hand above and one below). (See Plate 20)

This type of ground shot rarely comes as a direct shot, because these are usually one foot or so off the ground, but they do often occur when a winger cuts in and pulls a ball back into the area, and also when a goalkeeper has to dive at a forward's feet.

Diving at a Forward's Feet

Courage and fearlessness are key requirements of a goalkeeper. In no case do they apply more than when a goalkeeper has to dive at an oncoming forward's feet. But I would like to say that this action is not half as fearsome or dangerous as many people like to think. If done quickly and correctly, the likelihood of injury is very slight.

There are two methods of diving at or in front of an oncoming forward –
(1) head-on dive,
(2) side dive.

(1) The head-on dive is always thought of as the most dangerous save in goalkeeping. I dispute this and would place a side dive as more dangerous.

It occurs usually when an opposing forward has broken

Fig. 19. Diving at a forward's feet

through the defence. The goalkeeper must advance out of goal in order to narrow the angle. However, if the ball is a through ball or if the forward slightly over-dribbles it, then you must instinctively go down.

Instinctive is the most important word for a slight hesitation could result in injury or a goal. The thing to watch when going out is that you don't give the man half-a-chance to lob it over your head.

The 'keeper can often sense when the player bearing down on him has lost control for one yard only – and that yard brings into operation the combined speed of movement and fearless dive.

In diving at a forward's feet the goalkeeper reaches for the ball with both hands at full arms-length. The hands should come down on top of the ball and, as soon as contact is made, the ball is tucked into the body.

Speed and agility combined in pouncing on the ball make all the difference between success and failure. Perhaps the best exponents of this head-on dive were Bert Trautmann, (the former Manchester City 'keeper) and nowadays Tommy Lawrence of Liverpool and Scotland. (See Plate 5)

(2) The side dive, as I have said, is the most dangerous. This is because the ball is snatched into the body as the player's boot comes through; the latter follows through into the ribs. This type of dive is usually undertaken when the goalkeeper

has more time to go down. In the former it should only be a 'last ditch' effort.

The most important thing is to get down on to the ball before he kicks, so that, even if he cannot stop his kick, he will hit a firmly grasped ball and his foot will be stopped dead. As I have said, it is the follow-through which is the most dangerous aspect.

In the side dive two other methods can also be tried –

(a) With sufficient time, the goalkeeper should dive over the top of the ball, and so turn his back on the forward. The arms are bent as he dives over it, so encircling the ball. Now the ball and the front of the body are guarded from the forward and the ball is hugged to the chest.

(b) With less time, a side dive with the body parallel to the ground and facing the forward is used. The hope of the keeper then is that the ball is either shot against his hands, his legs or his stomach. On each of these the chances are the ball will rebound, although it is possible to hold it. Defenders must always be alive to the possibility of a rebound.

The number of times a goalkeeper dives at a forward's feet and saves a certain goal, without getting injured, proves my argument that the dive is not dangerous and in every way vital.

Approaching out of Goal (i.e., Anticipation and Narrowing the Angles)

The problems of when to leave the goal-line present ever-increasing difficulties to a young goalkeeper. But this is something he must practise and practise until he has a highly-developed sense of anticipation and is able to narrow the angle almost instinctively.

Of course, when the goalkeeper advances to the ball he has far less time in which to react to stop it. Therefore while developing his anticipation he must reduce his reaction time. The 'keeper is highly susceptible to a lobbed ball or a sideways pass or a dribble. Once you are good at narrowing the angle,

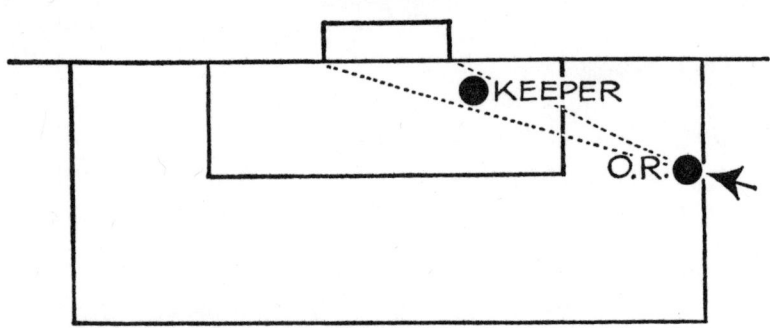

Fig. 20

however, you seem to give the forward no goal to aim at except your own body.

It is important, I feel, to explain narrowing the angle again and in slightly more detail. If we imagine that the goal-line between the goalposts is the permanent base of a triangle, then the changing vertex of this triangle is the position of the forward who is about to shoot.

The goalkeeper must place himself as in Figs. 20 and 21 so that his arms can almost touch both sides of the triangle. If the ball passes outside the sides of the triangle it will miss the goal.

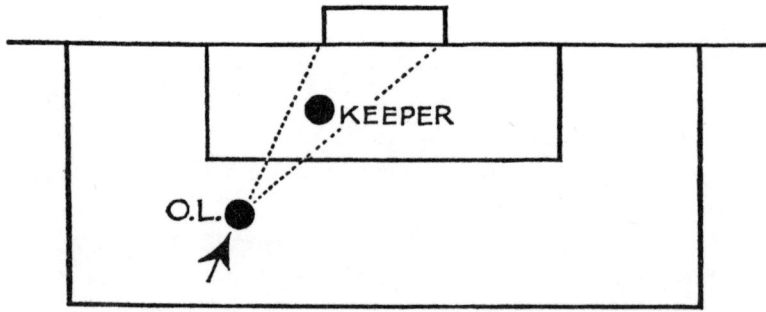

Fig. 21

ACCEPTED TECHNIQUES

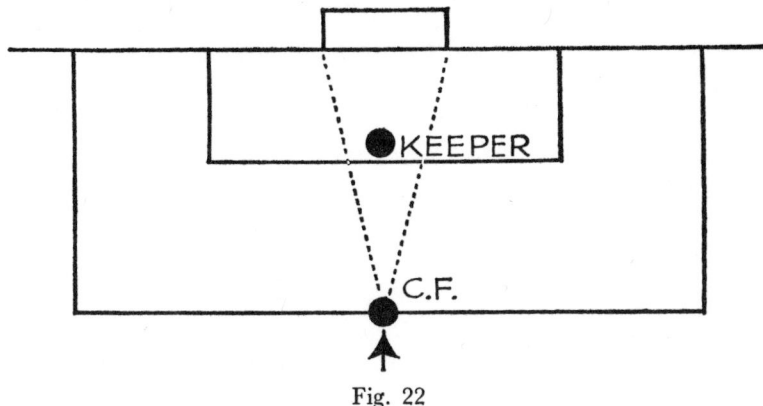

Fig. 22

In Fig. 20 the job is considerably easier though the goalkeeper has to guard against the possibility that the outside-right may do the sensible thing and centre.

In Fig. 21 the outside-left has more of a shooting angle. The 'keeper cannot cover the area entirely for if he is drawn too far out it is easy to lob him. But nevertheless by advancing a little he can make the uncovered area of the goal seem very small. It is far better to be bold and take a risk and in the majority of cases the risk will be a correct, calculated one.

When the ball is directly in front of goal (See Fig. 22), there is very little the 'keeper can do apart from advancing a little way and perhaps guess where the forward will play it.

In fact, in a breakaway the sole hope of saving a goal is by advancing to meet the forward, rather than letting him pick his spot. By coming out, the 'keeper makes the forward reconsider the correct moment to shoot or makes him wonder whether to dribble it around. This slight hesitation may give the keeper time to go down on his feet or the defence to recover. A chance to save is, therefore, created and the 'keeper must try and make himself as big and conspicuous as possible.

Penalties

A goalkeeper can comfort himself with the knowledge that

no man on earth can save a penalty kick which is properly placed. As well as that, the 'keeper should remember that the kicker is probably worrying far more, for everyone expects him to score.

However, the 'keeper cannot move his feet until the ball is touched and so the chance of saving depends on two factors—

(a) He guesses which way the ball will go and then goes for it by instinct.

(b) He hopes the taker will mishit or half-hit the ball.

The easiest to save are those three and four feet from the ground and a yard or two to the side.

Generally it is not difficult to tell where the shot is going. In an orthodox kick the run-up and backswing are in line with the ball's flight. Or you may know that the player has a favourite spot or side for his penalties. Even this knowledge should not enable you to save a well-taken penalty.

The kicker who tries to deceive the 'keeper with a body swerve offers more time to save. But then the 'keeper is generally to one side and the ball is entering the other.

Many 'keepers try to bluff, by standing far to one side of the goal, tempting the kicker to shoot at the other. Thus they will know precisely where to dive. But what they cannot control is the power of the shot, which is usually too great and too fast for them to do very much about it.

It seems a pity that one cannot resort to the antics of one Rab McFarlane. He would stand on his line and, as the opponent ran up to kick the ball, he would tear off his cap, whirl it round and bawl the most frightening gibberish. He also danced around to such an extent that the kicker was put off. However, so famous did this gift become that the rule, as it stands today, had to be drawn up.

My advice to a young goalkeeper would be to watch the penalty run-up and the position of the kicker's foot. It is often the only chance to save.

ACCEPTED TECHNIQUES

Passing Back

This is seldom a sign of weakness or panic but almost always a sign of good understanding and mutual confidence, though it must not be overdone.

It can be constructive in that the goalkeeper is in a position to see all his colleagues and has a certain amount of time to select where to make his pass, whereas the hard-pressed defender is almost certainly facing the wrong way and has little time to make a controlled pass. However, the goalkeeper must not be on the heels of the colleague, otherwise mistakes can occur, on a muddy, slippy ground.

Making a Clearance and Four-step Rule

In the last two years time-wasting by goalkeepers has been supposedly removed by the introduction of the four-step rule. Undoubtedly it makes the game more flowing, but it presents the 'keeper with a number of problems.

By practice you must learn to feint to throw the ball one way and make it as realistic as possible by also shouting the name of a team-mate. The opponent will almost certainly follow your action. A quick feint and you have that vital yard to kick away.

But beware the hastily booted clearance because you might easily miskick, especially by being forced on to your left foot. 'Keepers must practise kicking equally well with the left foot as with the right.

The dangers of the four-step rule are obvious to the 'keeper and can cause catastrophes such as befell Gary Sprake of Leeds in the 1968 F.A. Cup semi-final.

Sprake was forced on to his left foot at the extreme point of the 18-yard line and on the bye-line. He cleared hastily, miscued and the ball bounced to an Everton player, who promptly put it towards the goal where Jack Charlton was forced to handle and concede a penalty.

So Leeds were put out of the competition and all it involves as a direct result of this harsh rule that has placed an additional burden on the goalkeeper.

The 'keeper must now learn to make space whilst still keeping possession of the ball and keeping within the limits of the laws of the game.

The only chance a 'keeper has now of making ground to the edge of his box after having gained possession is to find an open route and roll and dribble the ball, preferably towards either of the two corners of the box.

Once there he should be composed enough to assess his outlets and deliver a quick throw upfield. Alternatively he can kick or, if as is often the case when his defence have been under pressure, he can 'hold' until he judges that his defence are well balanced and prepared for any event.

Problems occur immediately a forward 'stands on' a keeper with the ball. This is where the rule is farcical. If you are caught on your goal-line or on the by-line and hemmed in by an opponent, you then have to make a clearance from ridiculous positions.

Clearances – Throwing and Kicking

It is often said nowadays, and quite rightly, that the goalkeeper is not only the last line of defence but also the initiator of the attacks. This is done either by throwing the ball or kicking it.

Throwing

Since the great Frank Swift first realised the potential of throwing it has been developed to such an extent that nowadays a goalkeeper, during a match, will occasionally use it more than a kick. The fact is that a fair share should be given to both so that the opposition cannot know which type you are going to use.

There are two accepted types of throw :
(a) The Water-Polo Flick. (Fig 23)
(b) The Overarm Throw. (Fig 24)

Plate 1: The basic position for a goalkeeper (see chapter 3)

Plate 2: It's not always possible to catch the ball in a crowded goalmouth. Here Bob Wilson uses his fist to clear from the heads of Nottingham Forest forwards. (see chapter 3)

Plates 3 and 4: Bob Wilson shows how a goalkeeper should position himself to take a low shot (see chapter 3)

Plate 5: It can be a dangerous business diving at a forward's feet as this picture shows. Liverpool's Tommy Lawrence, who Bob Wilson rates as one of the bravest goalkeepers in the country, grabs the ball from the foot of Chelsea's Birchenall (see chapter 3)

Plate 6: Bob Wilson demonstrates an exercise which strengthens stomach muscles and punching ability (see chapter 5)

Plates 7, 8 and 9 (*left-hand page*) and 10 and 11 (*above*) illustrate how Bob Wilson quickens his reactions by having to lay flat by the post before a server throws or kicks the ball to the other side of the goal (see chapter 5)

Plates 12, 13 and 14 (*left-hand page*) and 15, 16 and 17 (*above*) and 18, 19 and 20 (*see over page*) show the sitting, kneeling and squatting positions in Bob Wilson's special training programme (see chapter 5)

Plate 21: England's Gordon Banks, who Bob Wilson rates as one of the best goalkeepers the country has ever produced, seen in action against Scotland at Wembley (see chapter 7)

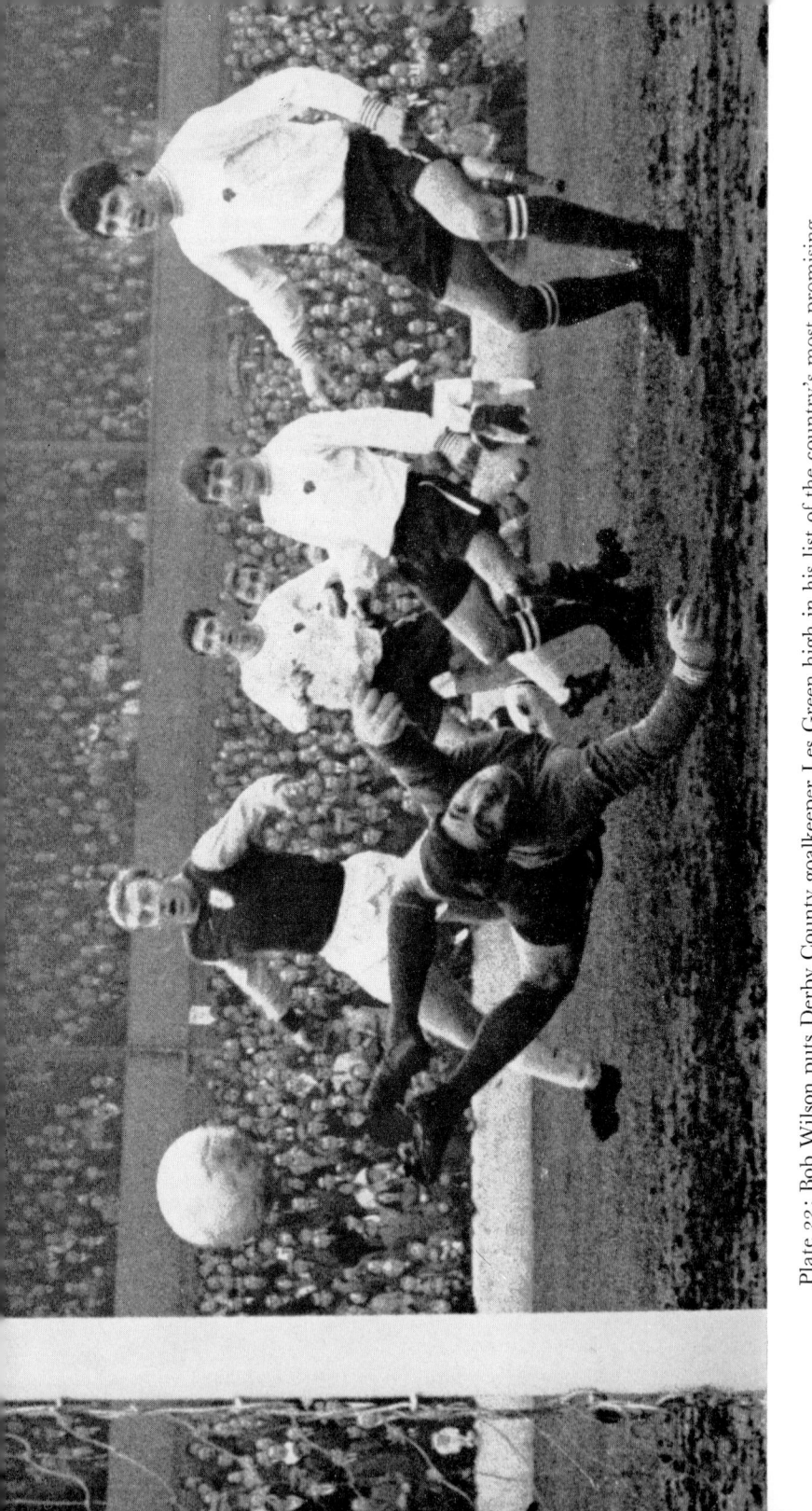

Plate 22: Bob Wilson puts Derby County goalkeeper Les Green high in his list of the country's most promising young 'keepers. Here Green makes a spectacular dive, but could not stop this free-kick from Burnley winger Dave Thomas from going into the net (see chapter 7)

ACCEPTED TECHNIQUES

Fig. 23. The water polo flick

(a) The Water-Polo throw has, as the name suggests, a great likeness to that game. It is used generally for any throw around the area or up to 25 yards. Its advantage is the impetus that it obtains and it is far more direct and accurate than the overarm. (Fig. 23)

It is also the throw that gets a goalkeeper out of trouble when he is challenged by a forward. The action is one of a bent arm, as in water-polo or basketball. The ball, held in the top of the hand, is drawn back in a straight line and in the direction to which it will travel. The bent arm is brought through and at its fastest point the ball is released, usually and helpfully being thrown at a colleague's feet. The left foot is advanced so that the weight of the body is evenly distributed. The grip is slightly relaxed.

(b) Overarm throws enable the 'keeper to send the ball almost as far as a kick and almost as accurately, if not more so. The ball is held by the hand and the waist, the other hand

GOALKEEPING

Fig. 24. The overarm throw

steadies it during the preliminary movement which begins to draw it backwards. The arm is carried back as the body turns sideways and the opposite leg swings forward. The throwing action is an overarm movement, very much like the bowling action in cricket. Indeed, the ball should, if there is no obstruction, be sent down to a player's feet. But the 'keeper has to be careful not to put spin on the ball, which is quite possible with this type of throw. (Fig. 24)

A final throw that is widely used for switching direction, but with a short range, is a simple under-arm throw.

Kicking

It used to be said that a kick was just an enormous boot up the field. Modern techniques put the emphasis on placing the ball from goal kicks and from kicks from the hand.

Goal Kicks: These are now the least accurate of any clearance. In the main they should be directed to either the wing or the centre-forward. The latter is often able to head the ball down to an inside forward who can split the defence by a through pass. Young goalkeepers must practise this dead ball kicking more than they do, for on muddy grounds they sometimes get it only just outside the area.

The best method of taking goal kicks is with the instep in the same way that forwards shoot at goal. The only difference is that you must loft the ball to some extent and there is not quite the same necessity to lean over the ball.

It is possible also to get quite a good long kick with the method used for long passes and corner-kicks, i.e. with the foot inclined at a slight angle. The only small disadvantage of this method is that your kick will go slightly higher and will lose a little distance by curling. But it is a good alternative if the instep method fails.

It is also best to take a reasonable run at the ball of about six-to-12 paces. The eye should be kept on the ball until kicked and the great secret of getting power is turning. Therefore it is advisable to run at the ball slightly from the side, not dead straight.

Whether you direct kicks to the wings or down the centre depends on circumstances. The method used depends on whether the opposition's centre-half is too strong for your centre-forward, or whether a full-back is weak. Generally the kick is based upon the ability and playing form of the opposition. And the goalkeeper can be the first to spot a weakness.

Other Clearances

Much the same applies to punting the ball. The goalkeeper must learn to punt with either foot, so that he is not limited either in the way he has to dodge forwards who rush him or in the direction in which he kicks the ball. A low flight is best for it enables a player to bring it under control easier.

When clearing in the course of a game the 'keeper will often have the opportunity to change the direction. For instance, if the opposition attacks down the right wing and the 'keeper gains possession, he can transfer it rapidly to the left wing.

GOALKEEPING

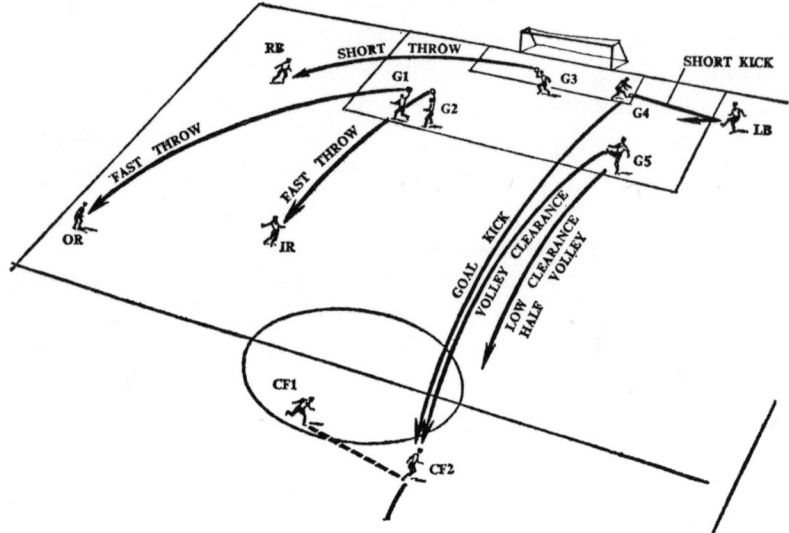

Fig. 25. Various types of clearance

A low drop kick provides a very acceptable pass to the attack, but this could only be undertaken when there is no chance of an interception. Keep the head well down and your eye on the ball until it is kicked.

Finally, when a goal-kick is taken it is now common to play the ball out of the penalty area to a full-back and then to receive it back so that the 'keeper may make use of his area before volleying upfield.

Conclusion

I would like to stress that no goalkeeper conforms strictly to these techniques in every game. Occasions and circumstances will arise that force him to make an improvised save.

For example, feet and legs and any part of the body has at times to be used as desperation methods. But, ungainly or not, if the ball is kept out of the net, then the 'keeper has done his job.

4. THE PSYCHOLOGY OF GOALKEEPING

Study of opponents (1) before the game (2) during the game – elimination of possibilities (1) reading the situation (2) forcing errors upon an opponent.

THE READER MAY BE SLIGHTLY SURPRISED AT A CHAPTER WITH such an educative title, but I believe that by the end of the chapter I will have shown that a goalkeeper does not avert goals purely by a fine save. The process begins before this, sometimes weeks before, and the preparation also calls for quick thinking and watching a player's habits in the early stages of a match.

The goalkeeper must learn to think hard in order to outwit opponents and anticipate their shots. This word, anticipation, has now been brought up several times already in the book to prove conclusively its importance in goalkeeping.

This outwitting of opponents can be done by various means. In the first place the goalkeeper can –

(a) *Study the Opponents* and study in particular the individual style of the opposing forwards. This should be done before a match, either by watching them in action against another team or by reading reports of matches in which they played a prominent part.

If one sees a future opponent hit a low ball to any one corner in a match, there is a good chance that he will repeat this tactic later. Knowledge is often the key to success and this knowledge can also be acquired by observing players closely during the actual course of a game. Whether they tend to use the outside or inside of the foot, whether the left or the right, and which is their favourite shot? All these can be noticed. Every footballer has certain habits and characteristics, and the goalkeeper can observe them during midfield play. He then tabulates them in his mind, and will be better prepared to react to a situation when his goal is threatened.

(b) *The Elimination of Possibilities* is the other main part of the psychology of goalkeeping. This involves reading the situation and forcing an opponent into errors. The battle is half-won if a goalkeeper is one move ahead of the forwards. During a game he can judge where the shot is coming, from the run of play initially and then by the backswing of the forward's foot. Only experience coupled with adequate practice will provide the knowledge of where the ball will go in relation to their feet.

I have found that a forward is inclined to drag the ball across goal if he hits it with his weaker foot. This anticipation comes from studying how forwards shoot at goal. A 'keeper can usually tell not just by the angle of the foot but by the position of the forward's body. The argument against it is that some forwards make a practice of pretending to put the ball to one side, hoping that the goalkeeper will prepare to move to that side. Then they kick it to the other side.

If the goalkeeper is deceived by the forward's action, it is almost certain that his weight is on one side, and it now becomes a difficult job transferring weight to the other. Once again, experience teaches a 'keeper to differentiate between the genuine shot and the false.

Sam Bartram, the ex-Charlton Athletic goalkeeper, wrote 'a goalkeeper should take risks provided, mind you, that they are justifiable risks'.

The goalkeeper must try to dictate a situation and force an opponent into errors. This is done normally by 'feinting' to one way, knowing full well that your weight is evenly balanced and you are going the other where you hope the shot will be hit.

The other way is to leave a gap to one side of the centre of the goalmouth, so that the forward aims at the opening you have deliberately left for him. This, as I have already mentioned, can be done from a penalty, and it equally applies if a forward is through by himself. But the 'keeper should not pin all his hopes on the forward doing as he wishes.

I recall how my idol, Bert Trautmann of Manchester City,

approached some four yards out of his goal as Mitchell, of Newcastle, moved towards the six-yard area in the 1954–55 F.A. Cup Final. At such an acute angle Trautmann prepared to dive outwards for the obvious kick-back, and left enough room to his right which he could have covered had he not based all his hopes on the ball being hit across. In fact, Trautmann recalls how Mitchell had previously not shot, but done the obvious.

He had done this in League games as well as during this Cup-Final. So, as Mitchell drew his foot back, Trautmann went to his left. To his amazement Mitchell hit it true and hard to his right and no more than a foot from Trautmann's outstretched right foot.

This provides the obvious moral that a 'keeper should not take everything he has seen before as gospel. Normally Trautmann's instinct would have paid him dividends, as indeed it did on many occasions during that same Cup-Final. Had he not taken the risk and Mitchell had pulled it back he would have been in just as awkward a position. Trautmann tried to make him do what he wanted, basing the gamble on previous knowledge, and the fact that he gambled and lost was better than being almost certainly lost had he stayed 'at home'.

Trautmann eliminated the chances of scoring to two, i.e. either a direct shot or a pull back to a forward. Then he brought it to one chance only. The fact that in this case he failed is beside the point. The goalkeeper must always try to eliminate the chances and reduce them to one only.

This case provides a prime example of eliminating possibilities and I need say no more. All other cases are similar and the way in which a goalkeeper reacts is shown in this example. As always, the answer to the problem is anticipation. On this basis the goalkeeper can then exercise his judgement and instincts, and the goalkeeper who knows his own abilities exactly and can judge the abilities of his opponents is not likely to make any of those foolish errors which result in a gift goal for the opponent.

GOALKEEPING

In my opinion this part of a goalkeeper's make-up is derived from an intelligent outlook on a game and after the game.

After every match I find time to sit and think about the game played. The game is, in fact, replayed and relived. My homework includes drawing up diagrams as accurately as possible to reproduce the line of attack leading up to the goals against me and the actual scoring attempt.

In such a manner I almost always can pin down just why the goal occurred. This is usually one of three reasons –

(a) – an unstoppable shot from a forward, and these do exist!

(b) – a mistake by a defender.

(c) – a mistake by the goalkeeper.

In the final case more attention must be paid to finding out why the mistake was made. This thorough analysis of your play helps to build experience and knowledge. This knowledge is instrumental in improving anticipation and positional play and coupled to both there should be the natural instincts and abilities that make a goalkeeper.

5. FUNCTIONAL TRAINING

Situation Training – Personal Training Programme – General Training – Exercises and Activities

General

IN CHAPTER 2, I COMMENTED HOW THE GOALKEEPER WAS OFTEN considered the least fit member of the team. As a ball-player I would possibly agree, but this he is not. Instead his fitness is specific. I should explain this by saying that beyond a general level of fitness the 'keeper builds himself or his body up for the specific art of goalkeeping. His agility and mobility exercises in training will be greater than the normal player, but his stamina could be less.

It is well to remember that he is not going to train much with the ball at his feet, but is going to develop and train his catching and handling ability. He is also going to spend much of his training in his goalmouth with the emphasis on goalkeeping situations. Only by hours of practice, moving about the goal, will the goalkeeper develop an accurate sense of his position in relation to the goal. In this chapter I find it more appropriate to break training into two parts:

(a) Situation training.
(b) General training.

Situation Training

Ball Handling: **Youngsters and even the more experienced professional 'keepers cannot get enough of straightforward basic handling. This can be done anywhere and at any time.**

Bouncing, throwing the ball against a wall and punching should be done over and over again for these exercises build up that abounding confidence which, if expressed by the goalkeeper in a game, will spread rapidly throughout the rest of the team. So every possible chance should be taken to brush up confidence by basic handling.

GOALKEEPING

These handling exercises can be done solo, but are probably best practised in pairs.

Examples:
(1) Bounce the ball at a wall or any flat surface and catch the rebound, either at arms-length or to the chest (Fig. 26). Concentrate on all basic goalkeeping techniques – i.e. good balance, on toes, eye on ball, mobility, getting body behind it, pulling it on to chest and holding securely.

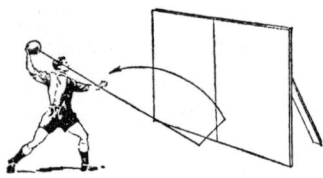

Fig. 26

(2) Kick the ball at wall or flat surface and dive to catch the rebound (Fig. 27). Can be done in a gym, or field with shooting board.

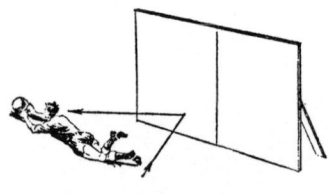

Fig. 27

(3) *In Pairs* – X throws and bounces the ball at Y who catches and returns it. Both try to trick each other by spinning the ball and throwing it at different heights and speeds (Fig. 28).

(4) X kicks at Y and follows it up. Y saves and dodges X.

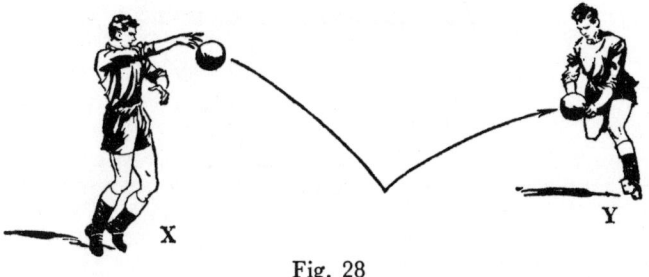

Fig. 28

(5) *In Threes* – X throws the ball to Y and follows up by attempting to charge Y who dodges (bouncing the ball every 4 steps) and then throws to Z, and follows it up (Fig. 29).

Fig. 29

Practices that can be done individually:
(a) Start with basic handling and, as confidence grows, vary the height and speed of delivery.
(b) Change throwing against wall to kicking.
(c) Punching with varying height and trajectory.
(d) Throwing – Water-Polo type, overarm, underarm – built up to hit targets against wall.
(e) Kicking : (1) dead balls, (2) half-volleys (3) full kick.

I cannot stress enough the vital importance of individual practice which, probably above all else, can boost a 'keeper's confidence.

Making quick saves

The ability to make a lightning save when all is lost is the dream of every 'keeper, whether beginner or expert. This

GOALKEEPING

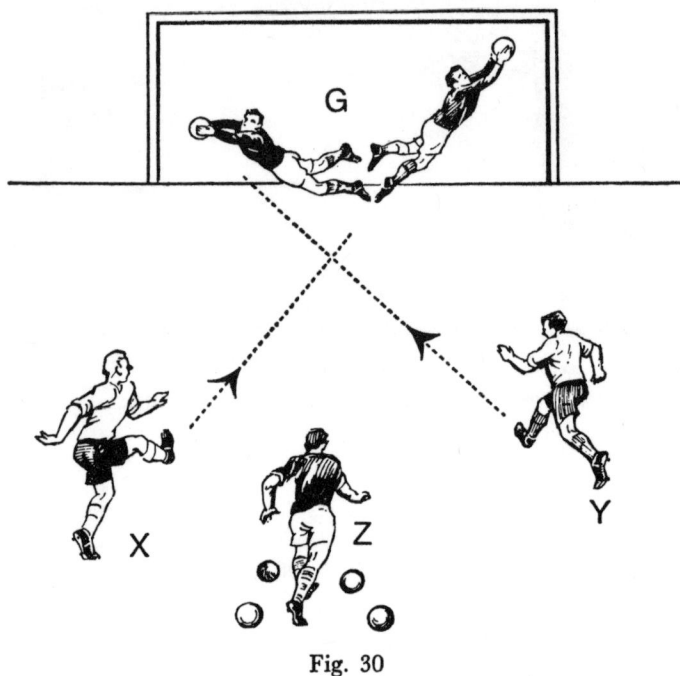

Fig. 30

ability is really a combination of anticipation and quick reaction as well as agility. One of the best ways of developing this skill is to practise making saves from close-in shots which follow each other fairly rapidly.

Exercise 1 (Fig. 30)

The goalkeeper (G) stands in goal. Two other players X and Y, each with a ball, prepare to shoot from some five yards away to left and right of the goal. Another player Z serves balls to X and Y when needed.

X shoots, placing the ball so that G can save it, but only by moving quickly. G rolls the ball back to X and this is the signal for Y to shoot, again placing the ball within G's reach. G rolls the ball back to Y and quickly turns to save the next shot from X and so on.

FUNCTIONAL TRAINING

Fig. 31

Sometimes a ball should be shot fiercely but directly at G to test his sureness in catching. But the main aim is to keep the goalkeeper, bending, stretching, jumping and diving from side to side, striving to stop each ball in turn. This activity provides fitness training of exactly the right type for goalkeepers.

Exercise 2 (Fig. 31)

This time G watches the ball coming into goal only to find it is deflected by another player near to goal. Again G has only a brief moment to react and catch or stop the ball.

The ball can be headed to either post and either in the air or down on the ground. Also the 'keeper can come out and intercept if he is able to, but X can lob directly into goal if this is made obvious.

Fig. 32

Exercise 3

IN PAIRS – Partner stands five yards out of goal and throws a ball for the goalkeeper to save. After he has saved one ball, a second ball is thrown. The throwing and saving is kept up continuously. This exercise can be done with the partner kicking instead of throwing.

Exercise 4

A very good practice within the gym or against any wall is one where the server stands directly behind the goalkeeper – Fig. 32. In this way the goalkeeper does not see the ball until it almost hits the wall and a reaction save is called for. The speed and height of the throw by the server is varied.

Diving on the ball

As I have stressed great courage and fearlessness are needed to dive at a player's feet. But this skill can be practised by a player bringing the ball through and delaying his shot. In this way the goalkeeper gains confidence in going down at a forward's feet.

Practice 1

The practice will follow the lines of the above statement. The forward should approach from different angles, and either keep

FUNCTIONAL TRAINING

Fig. 33 (i)

the ball at his feet until challenged or overkick it slightly, so giving the 'keeper a brief chance so capitalise on his mistake.

Practice 2 (Fig. 33)

The goalkeeper can combine this practice by diving over the ball to screen it from the opponent (Fig. 33, No. 1). Then he

Fig. 33 (ii)

gets to his feet, with his back to the opponent and feints to go in one direction (ii) but quickly turns and goes another way.

Dealing with an attack from the wing

One of the most dangerous attacking situations occurs when the winger runs into the penalty area with the ball (Fig. 34).

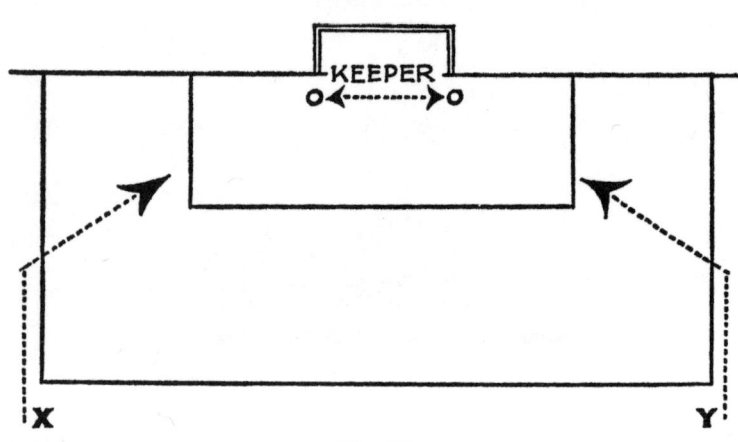

Fig. 34

The goalkeeper must cover the near post against a shot at goal. And he must also be ready to leap to the far post to catch a lob or even more quickly to the middle of the goal to guard against a shot, when the wingman pulls the ball back at an oblique angle.

Practice

The two wingers (X and Y) take turns to make an approach. Each chooses what he will do at the end of his run and G tries to prevent a goal.

The high ball

A goalkeeper must be agile and clever in saving shots at goal, but he will be a better goalkeeper if he can leave his goal safely and collect high balls which drop in and around his goal area. In this way he will be able to prevent a lot of danger to his goal that might arise if the ball came too near.

The skill of taking a high ball safely needs a lot of practice before the goalkeeper can be sure about timing and safe handling. The following are ways in which it can be practised:

(a) The players throw and catch. One player throws the ball with one hand overhead; the other player catches it with upstretched arms. At the limit of a jump (the jump should be from a single foot take-off). The hands should be slightly behind the ball and the body leaning forward a little.
(b) This time one player stands in position in goal and when he runs out to catch the ball from a long kick he quickly hugs it to his body and weaves his way, bouncing the ball as though dodging opponents.
(c) The high service to the goalkeeper should be varied so that sometimes the ball drops near the cross-bar. In this case the goalkeeper will use the palm of his hand or hands to push or turn the ball over.
(d) The ball can be kicked from well downfield or from near the corners and it is helpful to let another player challenge the goalkeeper either by jumping to head the ball or by charging him when the ball is in his grasp.
(e) The goalkeeper should arrange with his defenders so that they know when to take the ball themselves and when to drop back to cover the goal and leave the high ball to him.

As these are practised the 'keeper will gradually learn when he can safely leave the goal and when he should stay on the line.

Low shots

This difficult type of shot is practised not only with the ball but without it. Former England 'keeper Ron Springett explains: 'I spend some of my training stopping imaginary low shots from various angles.' This is called shadow goalkeeping and not only does it condition the 'keeper to fall correctly, but also enables him to get down quicker. The ideal practice for getting down to low shots is gained by having one ball served up within reach of the goalkeeper and another where the ball is hit low to left and to right. But I would stress agility, work and training, particularly in the case of the tall goalkeeper. This is essential if he is to get down to the low shots.

GOALKEEPING

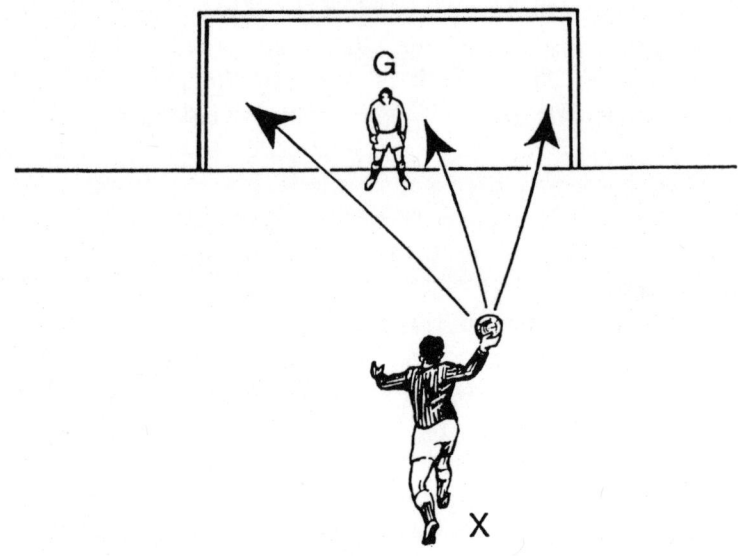

Fig. 35

Throwing the ball

A goalkeeper's throw should be a feature of his play. It is more accurate than a dead ball kick and can be thrown considerable distances.

Exercises

Goalkeepers can practise throwing in pairs. G and X first stand three yards apart and throw single-handed with the 'push' throw. Each arm is used in turn for throwing (this helps in fitness) and the throw is aimed at the partner's chest. Sometimes the ball is thrown down at the ground but other types of throw can be used.

Gradually G and X increase the distance between them until they are as far apart as they can throw, using the best throwing arm.

Fig. 35: X throws high balls to G, so that he has to meet it by running forward, G then throws it as if he were setting up

FUNCTIONAL TRAINING

Fig. 36

an attack to the inside-forward or a player during a match. (Fig. 36)

Fig. 37: This type of exercise has a dual purpose. A third player (preferably a goalkeeper) Y joins G and X. G is in goal and X and Y stand near each touch-line as wingmen. X bounces the ball and kicks it to G. In this way he tests his accuracy of kick, whether it be a dead ball, a volley or a half-volley. G fields the ball, preferably with a high catch, turns and sends a long throw out to Y who catches the ball and kicks it back to G.

Practice covering all points

In this activity the goalkeeper has to face a series of different

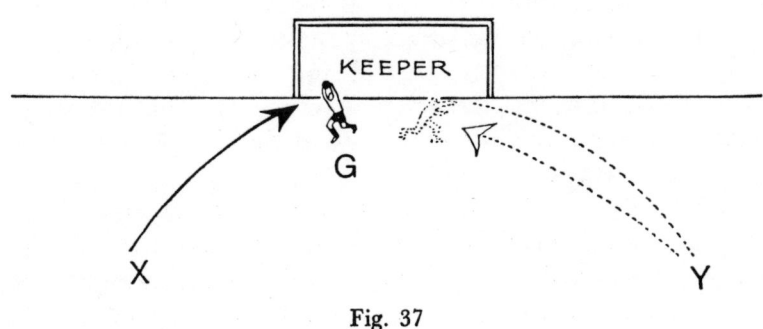

Fig. 37

GOALKEEPING

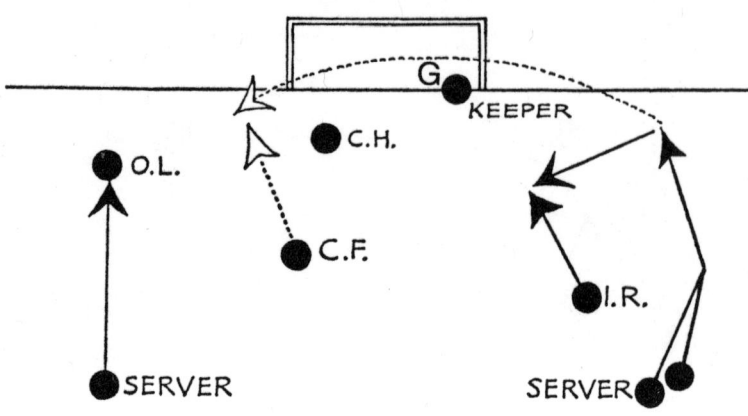

Fig. 38

situations to which he must react as quickly and as well as he can.

This practice is illustrated in Fig. 38.

G (the goalkeeper) positions himself in goal ready to meet the first attack which comes from a winger running in towards the goal-line. G must obviously come to the near post and he must react to be ready to –

(a) stop a shot from the right-winger,

(b) dive to cut out a fast low centre if he is near enough to it,

(c) jump high to catch a lobbed ball.

This practice again has various adaptations such as two balls being used at once.

If the right-winger succeeds in lobbing the ball too high to be caught, G must turn and position himself to cover the other end of his goal against an attack by the centre-forward.

If G catches or saves the ball and the inside-right moves to challenge him, the 'keeper must evade him and throw the ball to the server on the other side of the field who positions himself as a wingman.

Having dealt with this first attack, G now prepares to deal with a lobbing centre from the outside-left. He has to judge the situation whether to go out of goal to make a high catch or to leave his centre-half to deal with the centre-forward while he covers the goal. These attacks alternate from right and left with the 'keeper and the centre-half constantly assessing what to do.

Each goalkeeper has his particular problems and weaknesses. If he is to improve his all-round ability, he must work at these phases of play and skill until he feels confident to face up to them in a real game.

My training programmes and contents

I practise the following type of exercises and activities, varying the programme and the sessions, which are held usually on Tuesdays and Thursdays. The sessions last for approximately 20 minutes and are carried out non-stop, with everything done in rapid sequence.

(a) *Sitting facing server*

The ball is served rapidly to the sides, above, in front of and beyond. The 'keeper *must* catch everything and the exercise develops reactions, handling and suppleness. It also strengthens stomach muscles as the 'keeper has to pull himself back from fully lying positions. (Plates 12, 13, 14)

(b) As above, but the 'keeper this time is in *kneeling* position and has to lift himself from this position.

This practice is useful in that quite often in a game a 'keeper parries a ball and then his reaction will decide whether he saves or is beaten. This has to be done by picking himself off his knees. (Plates 15, 16, 17)

(c) As above, but this time the 'keeper is in squatting position.

All exercises are done rapidly to improve agility and build up leg strength. (Plates 18, 19, 20)

(d) As above, but in a lying position. This is a pure brute strength exercise and aids the 'keeper once again in picking himself off the ground after he has parried one shot.

The server can push the 'keeper to right or left and, as in all these exercises, the 'keeper must catch everything if possible.

(e) As above, but in full standing basic position. The server does not try to beat the 'keeper but pushes him to the limits of his reach.

As in all the exercises, the 'keeper should try to gather and hold on to the ball.

In his final position, which is of course nearest to a match situation, the server will vary his angles, his speed of service and generally go through all positions of importance.

(f) Lying facing server, who throws the ball for the 'keeper to punch straight back to him as powerfully as possible. (Plate 6)

(g) Server throws the ball from distance and dictates whether the 'keeper catches or punches, by a shout.

(h) Goalkeeper at the near post. Server either tries to beat him inside or forces him out to cut out low cross.

(i) As above, but server throws ball high so that the 'keeper has to deflect it, either single-handed or two-handed, over the bar.

Before I progress on to general training it must be made clear that situation training exercises are endless in their variety and number. I could go on making up exercises for goalkeepers for quite some time, but my purpose in this chapter is to show the main ones from which a great deal of adaptation can take place. I have also tried to stress that the goalkeeper's training is very different from that of a midfield player. I hope you now appreciate the importance of functional training and, in particular, pressure training.

General Training

I have briefly mentioned that a goalkeeper has a basic level of fitness as well as his specific fitness. The basic fitness he gains from doing a regulated amount of stamina training and running, as done by the outfield players, and also from playing other games. The best tests for goalkeeping are those that develop speed, eye on the ball and, to some extent, agility.

Five-a-side

In this game, often played within the club's training session or by schoolboys, the goalkeeper should not play in goal but as a forward. In this way he improves his speed and becomes aware of the problems of a forward when he is faced by a goalkeeper. This is part of the psychology of goalkeeping in being able to quickly put yourself into the forward's position and read what he is going to do.

Squash

This game is magnificent for goalkeeping in that it aids speed, agility and mobility, and stamina. More than any other game, squash speeds up your reactions. The problem is that there are too few squash courts.

Tennis is another useful exercise for goalkeepers. Table tennis, fives, basket ball, which is superior to squash in some ways, especially in that a ball is used and catching and handling are prominent. The fact that you are not under as much pressure as in squash is only a slight disadvantage.

Golf

Having thought considerably about the use of this game as an aid, I now believe it has some purpose. Not only does it clear the cobwebs and worries as one walks from hole to hole, and relieves tension, but it also gives the goalkeeper and other players an understanding of the eye and ball relationship.

All these sports have a place in the general fitness of a goalkeeper and should be planned and brought into not only pre-season training but also mid-season training.

Exercises

Exercises are used today mostly to warm-up and stretch, but for goalkeepers can be used appropriately to increase mobility and suppleness. Rolling activities and hip flexion and extension and rotation in particular are useful, as indeed are exercises designed to mobilise the shoulder girdle and leg joints.

GOALKEEPING

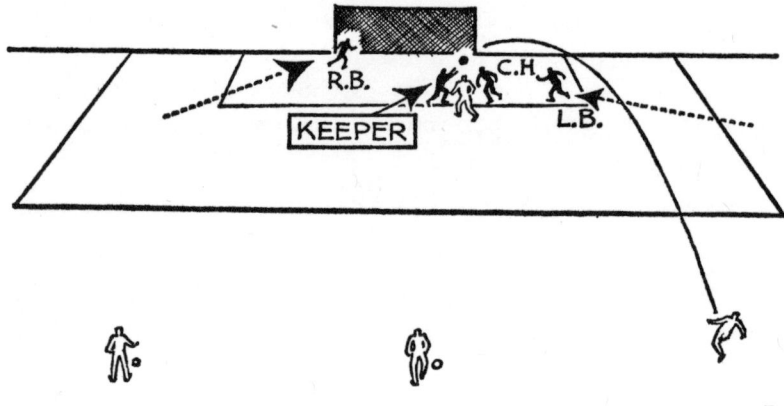

Fig. 39

Examples of shoulder exercises
Arm circling, arm pressing, full press.

Hip exercises
Trunk Curls, rotation of hip.

Leg exercises
Numerous forms of jumping, especially bunny jumping (for leg strength), back lying, leg raising, squat jumps.

These are but a few of the many, but give the purpose and place of exercises within a goalkeeper's training.

Another most important aspect of a goalkeeper's training is the need to build up an understanding with his fellow defenders. More importantly, there must be great co-operation with the centre-half and two full-backs.

It is useful in practice to produce a sequence of attacking situations which are similar to those of a game.

(1) The goalkeeper and three defenders are in the penalty area (Fig. 39). The ball is then lobbed into the area and either the goalkeeper or his defenders make a clearance and so they get to know what type of centre the goalkeeper will go for,

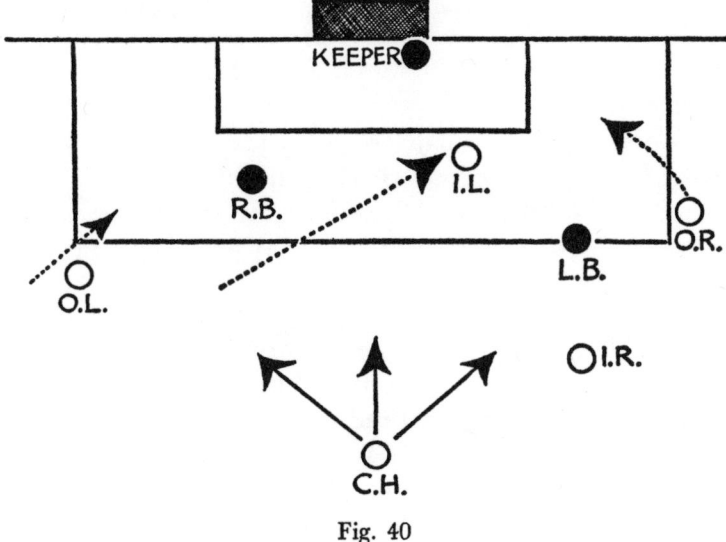

Fig. 40

his different calling and whether or not they should go to clear.

(2) (Fig. 40) It is interesting to see if the three defenders and goalkeeper can counter a series of attacks from a full forward line. They attack as in a game and if the defenders win possession a new wave of attack begins. In this way a defensive pattern is created and different types of attack will test the goalkeeper's ability to come out or stay put.

Other related practices include throwing and goal-kicks. I have already mentioned throwing, but goal-kicking is something that a 'keeper must practise alone or with a fellow goalkeeper and experiment in practice games or full training sessions.

Free kicks

The types generally used have already been described and the practice of these kicks takes place during training sessions. It is futile to just talk about them and then put them into practice in matches. Instead the defence as a whole must practise and practise until all situations can be faced.

Penalties

This practice is often indulged in by players at the end of a training session, and is somewhat lighthearted. It should, however, be treated seriously and organised to give the goalkeeper experience in the different types of penalty and also real practice in saving.

Other activities incorporated in general training

(1) The goalkeeper is positioned on the edge of the six-yard line. Other players are stationed on the edge of the 18-yard line with a ball. On a signal from the coach the players, in turn, try to chip the ball over the 'keeper into the net. The 'keeper is required to use all his speed and agility whilst moving backwards to save.

(2) The goalkeeper is lying down touching the post at full stretch. The players are again on the edge of the box with a ball. On a given signal the player tries to score and the 'keeper meanwhile has to pick himself off the ground and try to save. (Plates 7, 8, 9, 10, 11) Then he goes down again and the exercise is repeated. (See picture strip opposite page 64)

(3) Goalkeeper is positioned in goal. The forwards play the ball up to a target man who lays it off and the forwards shoot at goal. The 'keeper must attempt to save.

I hope that I have managed to convey to the reader an idea of the variety and specific nature of a goalkeeper's training. The exercises in this chapter should be arranged and planned according to the time of the year and the needs of the individual.

It is essential that each exercise should gradually introduce the conditions of a real game, and that the goalkeeper should put everything into his practice as though a game were in progress. Only in this way will he develop the right type of reaction and timing and gain experience.

6. INTRODUCTION OF GOALKEEPING IN SCHOOL

Games from primary school age up to secondary school age.

WHEN TEAMS ARE PICKED FOR A GAME OF FOOTBALL AT SCHOOL or in the park, the same old question of 'who is going in goal' occurs. This is natural as, in the park game, he can be somewhat left out. And the boy doesn't yet realise that, in fact, the goalkeeper is the most specialised man in a team, being the last line of defence and the first line of attack.

The question of introducing goalkeeping to a primary school boy is difficult, for at that age he is boundless in energy, impressed by all he sees and unless he has a very unusual aptitude for the position the last place he will want to go is in goal. The problem is further complicated by the shortage of sufficiently enthusiastic teachers who could introduce goalkeeping to a primary schoolboy.

However, in my opinion, the positions in football should be made clear to the boys at this early age and goalkeeping should be no exception. They should be introduced as a group activity and in such a way are readily enjoyable.

The first group practice will indicate that only a small contingent show the characteristics needed by a good 'keeper. In the first sessions ball-handling games are played, often in the form of introductory activities. These are followed by a class activity concerned with collecting the rolling ball in a stationary position. These practices progress to moving towards a rolling ball, moving away and behind and eventually to diving for the ball which cannot be reached in time to get well behind it.

The pattern for demonstration and activity should be as follows:

1. *Getting behind the ball*
    (i) Demonstration by teacher. (Fig. 41)
    (ii) In pairs. Rolling the ball to each other and collecting.

GOALKEEPING

Fig. 41

(iii) Kicking to partner, collect or 'gather'.
(iv) Low drive – move behind and collect.

2. *No. 1 in a game setting* (i.e. getting behind ball and saving)
These practices are to be continued in group manner, dividing the class into pairs, or whatever number the functional practice calls for. (Fig. 42)

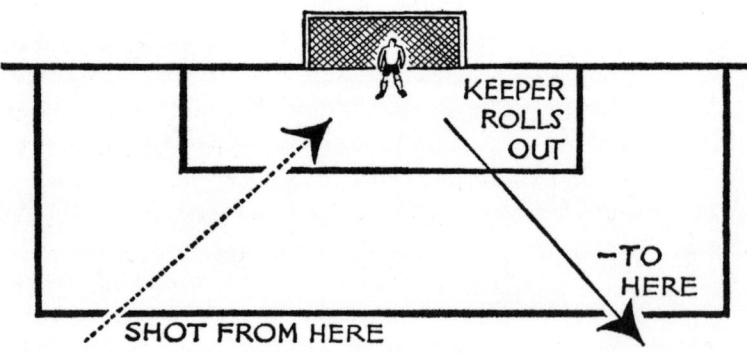

Fig. 42

INTRODUCTION OF GOALKEEPING IN SCHOOL

LOW DRIVES FROM DIFFERENT POSITIONS

Fig. 43

In Fig. 43 the aim of the exercise is to make the goalkeeper move out or across to gather the ball correctly.

3. *Narrowing the angle*

Only one practice need be used for this skill, the goalkeeper having to cover ground to lessen the gap for shots at goal by oncoming forwards. (Fig. 44)

Several other functional practices can easily be devised as long as the boy gathers the ball and positions himself correctly.

This is quite sufficient material to teach to the seven to

Fig. 44

10-year-old as a goalkeeper. Other coaching should be incidental. A boy might catch a ball wrongly, and here the coach must explain the correct way to catch a ball in the air.

At this stage tuition in diving, punching and diving at a forward's feet or falling on the ball should be avoided unless a boy asks for explanation or is in obvious need of such coaching. In all events the coach (or teacher) should use discretion. Otherwise one should limit the goalkeeping practices to the above in an effort to give the child just a piece of the cake without allowing him 'to bite off more than he can chew'. This applies to all functional practices carried out by primary school children.

As a team game in primary school, the small group games are most suitable and five-a-side is the most appropriate.

Five-a-side

It enables everyone to be in the game all the time and soon gives the observer the knowledge he requires as to who is good and who is not so good. Also, the goalkeeper in a five-a-side game is –

(a) Constantly in the game;

(b) doesn't suffer from charging or fear of charging;

(c) doesn't have to dive at a forward's feet;

(d) he has a limited goal, as compared to a full sized goal, and therefore has a better chance of saving;

(e) he gains great satisfaction and interest in being the saver of goals;

(f) he learns how to distribute by underarm throws and water-polo throws.

Goalkeepers are gradually selected from groups and, with proper encouragement, the boy will retain his interest in goalkeeping until he reaches secondary school. Discretion must be used in teaching the basic skills of goalkeeping so that the boy will have a foundation upon which to build by the time he arrives at secondary school.

The gradual development, if the above policy is followed,

INTRODUCTION OF GOALKEEPING IN SCHOOL

should be quite easy. If a boy is obviously an interested and promising goalkeeper, the coach or teacher must emphasise it to him.

Frank Swift once wrote: 'If you want to keep goal, fit yourself as well as you can for the job' and he followed it by seven points of the greatest importance.

These seven points should be explained to the boy or they should be put up on the school notice board for him to read. (See page 103)

Fig. 45

INTRODUCTION OF GOALKEEPING IN SCHOOL

(1) Keep your eye on the ball and your body behind it.

(2) Profit by your own mistakes. Hold an 'inquest' on all shots which beat you.

(3) Reach an understanding with the whole of the team not just the full-backs.

(4) Learn to call to your defence; don't be afraid to ask them for the return or back pass. It's one of the best moves in the game.

(5) Vary your goal kicks and clearances.

(6) Get it firmly fixed in your mind that when the ball is in the six-yard area it is yours.

(7) Watch and study top line goalkeepers – I learned that way.

Frank Swift faithfully adhered to these principles and they helped to make him a great 'keeper. They will also go a long way towards helping the young schoolboy to learn the art of goalkeeping.

7. IN RETROSPECT

Great Goalkeepers

BETWEEN 1905 AND 1920 THERE EXISTED PERHAPS THE GREATEST of all goalkeepers. He was Sam Hardy from my home town Chesterfield, who played his finest games with Aston Villa and England. He outshone even the achievements of Harry Hibbs and Frank Swift. His most notable assets were his perfect positioning and angling. The late Charles Buchan recalled how, in 1913, after suffering a leg injury, Hardy lost his mobility, but his uncanny anticipation enabled him to defy all the efforts of the Sunderland attack and helped win the F.A. Cup for Aston Villa, the score being 1–0.

Next to Sam Hardy, and incidentally very close to him in ability and similarity of play, was Harry Hibbs of Birmingham City. His secret, he said, was his art of anticipation, like Hardy. This indeed should be a lesson to all budding 'keepers.

Hibbs built up a knowledge of most players and if he was facing a raw recruit he would leave a yawning gap to one side and inevitably force the player to shoot there, to his own great satisfaction.

These two, Hardy and Hibbs, were evidently the greatest and I believe it was because they made things appear so simple. Goalkeeping in more recent years, particularly since the Continental teams started to bring their showy teams here just before the war, has moved into the Palladium spectacular class. Today it is questionable whether Hibbs or Hardy would get into a representative team. They weren't showy enough!

A modern 'keeper who displayed showmanship as well as brilliant play was Frank Swift of Manchester City. When told of this showmanship, Swift retorted: 'Oh, well I had to throw a bit in to please the crowd. Football is only a game after all.'

This was a typical remark by the genial giant, who amazed

everyone in that, at the height of 6 ft. 3 in., he was so agile and was as adept at saving ground shots as he was in catching high balls. In assessing Frank Swift, his ability is best explained by the fact that he must have been outstanding to keep out 'keepers of the calibre of Bert Williams of Wolves and Ted Ditchburn of Spurs.

All the 'keepers mentioned are English. In the other home countries only Elisha Scott of Liverpool and Northern Ireland and Jack Kelsey of Arsenal and Wales could match up to the class of Hardy, Hibbs and Swift.

These 'keepers had 'simplicity and safety' as their motto. What a contrast to the Continentals. Excellent as they were and are in some skills, their exhibitionism rates them lower in my opinion.

The first of the notable foreign 'keepers to appear was Hiden of Austria who impressed and delighted against England in 1932. Since then Beara of Yugoslavia, Grosics of Hungary and Yashin of Russia have been the best, each combining undoubted athletic prowess and ability with the showmanship that is part of world football. All these Continentals were showy but none so much as Olivieri, the pre-war Italian 'keeper.

If I may quote from the writing of John Macadam, he described Olivieri in these terms:

'Nothing was too easy for Olivieri to make look difficult. A simple pass back from one of his defenders and Olivieri tensed every muscle in his body, gathered himself like the clouds on Snowdon, coiled – and struck. He would leap high in the air, flatten out, describe a graceful parabola and then sweep on the inoffensive ball with the venom of a stoat fastening on a rabbit.

'Then with a magnificent gesture he would bound to his feet, run to the edge of the penalty box, and kick the ball out of sight – straight up in the air.' This may be a slight piece of exaggerated sports writing, but it emphasises Olivieri as the biggest clown goalkeeping has ever known.

Goalkeeping is one position in which English play has improved. Nothing has been lost in fielding, catching or clearing a ball. If long kicks are an advantage, then something has been gained. The constructive side of goalkeeping has certainly advanced. People like Swift and Ditchburn gave vent to the now familiar realisation that the 'keeper is not only the last line of defence but also the instigator of attacks.

My own idol, and the man I based my play on, was former Manchester City goalkeeper Bert Trautmann. He had all the qualities of a world-class goalkeeper and didn't appear to have any weaknesses. He was great on crosses, spectacular on his goal-line and was, perhaps, the bravest and best at coming off his line.

Trautmann was fantastic at diving at people's feet. The number of times I saw him do it was absolutely phenomenal. It resulted in him breaking his neck in the F.A. Cup final in 1956. If you had asked him if this terrible injury was worth it he would almost certainly reply that 'Yes it was, the ball didn't go in the net.' He was without doubt a natural. And I think basically a goalkeeper must have a natural talent to become outstanding. He has to have the ability to throw himself around instinctively without any thought of getting hurt.

Chelsea's Peter Bonetti, so agile and acrobatic, and Leicester's Peter Shilton, who has incredible confidence and a real bounce about his play, are ideal examples of really natural goalkeepers. Bonetti on his day looks the best and most stylish goalkeeper in English football. Shilton always has good control in his box and as a youngster has plenty of time to improve.

Everton's Gordon West, like Bonetti an England international, looks one of the best and most consistent goalkeepers in the First Division. Full of confidence, although I've read that he is often physically sick before a game, he is terrific on crosses.

Both Bonetti and West excel at throwing the ball out to their team-mates – but you're only as good as your players make you in this respect. In other words they must run into positions for you. A goalkeeper often has the choice of four players to throw to because, not only do the full-backs take up positions, but both wingers come back as well. Nevertheless, Bonetti and West are exceptional in this department.

England's first choice goalkeeper Stoke City's Gordon Banks, again an ex-Chesterfield player, is without doubt one of the greatest goalkeepers this country has ever seen. I think he, more than anybody, makes a save look easy – he never goes out of his way to make it spectacular and therefore can be likened to Hardy and Hibbs. Of course, at times he is spectacular because he is forced into a save that probably other 'keepers would be unable to make. In the World Cup I think he reached his highest peak; he was superb. Several other countries would have progressed further in the competition if they had a Banks in goal.

I would also like to mention Tommy Lawrence of Liverpool, whom I consider one of the bravest goalkeepers in the modern game. And bravery is such an important part of goalkeeping.

There are many up-and-coming goalkeepers such as David Best (Ipswich), John Jackson (Crystal Palace) and Les Green (Derby County), all of whom could become big names in the future.

As far as Continental goalkeepers are concerned, Simeonov (Bulgaria) looks the most recent 'discovery' following his incredible display against England recently. He now appears to be the eye-catcher.

But I think there are ten or eleven goalkeepers in England who could play in Continental national sides, and be the number one choice. This country produces more good goalkeepers at professional level than any other.

Now at last most goalkeepers, instead of just doing their normal training, realise that they are specialists and therefore train accordingly. I do normal training with the rest of the lads but at least twice a week I have my own goalkeeping sessions which I have illustrated in Ch. 5.

Keeping goal can be a great strain on the nerves. Other players can go looking for the ball but a goalkeeper, particularly in home matches, can be out of action for ten or fifteen minutes at a time. And that one vital moment, unless you concentrate 100 per cent, could lead to a goal.

When I come off the field, even when I have not had much to do, I feel really tired. My Arsenal team-mate Frank McLintock has told me that when he was at Leicester they used to make a joke out of the fact that Gordon Banks often said he was 'Absolutely exhausted'. But it's a mental tiredness rather than physical in most cases. You can be physically tired after hurling yourself around and taking a hammering, which you do occasionally, but generally it's 80 per cent mental stress, the concentration and build-up etc.

The goalkeeper is in the most unpredictable position on the field. You know the variety of shots and incidents that can happen but you never know in what order. You have to be prepared for everything the opposition can do, plus deflections off your own men, which occur through packed defences.

Probably the most nerve-racking aspect to overcome in your own mind is that for 89 minutes you might be a hero and then make a ridiculous boob, in the last minute whereas mistakes by outfield players can often be covered by colleagues. You can also make a terrible error in the first few minutes and have got to forget the crowd, which I don't think bothers top goalkeepers too much, and concentrate on the rest of the match. It has still to be won.

Twenty-four hours before a match I try to get my mind off it but do sometimes build up a mental picture of the opposition. Say it was West Ham: you can expect Geoff Hurst to be around ready to have a shot, Jimmy Greaves poaching, Bobby Moore will occasionally hit a blinder, and Harry Redknapp hits awkward crosses. But while I might conjure this up in my mind I don't dwell on it.

The bigger the crowd, the better the atmosphere and the less difficult it is to concentrate. I hate to play before an end-of-season crowd of about 14,000 with empty seats all round the place. It's like reserve team football – then you've got to try to build your own atmosphere and imagine you are playing at Wembley.

It's a big jump from the reserves to the first team, yet I found in some aspects the game was easier at top level. The crowd and the atmosphere probably helped. The biggest problem is knowing that you are going to make mistakes when you first go into the senior side because it is so different. The manager and coach should understand this and give you the opportunity to settle down. You must have time to acclimatise, especially today with packed defences. The rest of the team have got to know how you play and you've got to know all about them.

In modern football the main problems are on the physical side. When you are under pressure you hope your own defence does not retreat inside the 18-yard box, for you then run the risk of being unsighted. Areas do get packed, of course, from dead ball situations – corner-kicks, free-kicks etc. In these cases a goalkeeper must somehow find space and in many cases he will have to take up a false position. After that it is courage, speed of movement and determination to get to the ball.

In my opinion goalkeepers are worth every bit in the transfer market as the inflated prices paid for forwards. And I don't think it will be long before we have the first £100,000 goalkeeper. It's not an unreasonable view when you consider that a game can swing one way or another on the display of the goalkeeper.

For some reason the game just does not rate goalkeepers in the same price-range as outfield players. I'm not sure whether it's because there are so many good goalkeepers about or that the good ones are hard to buy.

Whatever the case I hope I have illustrated that although many might still feel one has to be slightly crazy to be a goalkeeper, they will at least recognise there is reason behind the apparent 'madness'.